GARNISHES, RELISHES, AND SAUCES

GARNISHES, RELISHES, AND SAUCES

FOR
FOODSERVICE
MENU
PLANNING

**Selected
by
EULALIA C. BLAIR**

Jule Wilkinson, Editor

Published by
CBI PUBLISHING COMPANY, INC.
221 Columbus Ave., Boston, Massachusetts 02116

Library of Congress Cataloging in Publication Data
Main entry under title:

Garnishes, relishes, and sauces for foodservice menu
   planning.

   (Foodservice menu planning series)
   Includes index.
   1. Cookery (Garnishes)   2. Cookery (Relishes)
3. Sauces.   4. Quantity cookery.   I. Blair,
Eulalia C.
TX652.G37   641.8'1   77-3292
ISBN 0-8436-2173-7

ISBN 0-8436-2173-7

*Cover Picture: Spanish Green Olive Commission; Pickle
Packers International; Apricot Advisory Board; Brussels
Sprouts Marketing Program, and National Cherry Growers
and Industries Foundation*

Printed in the United States of America

Contents

Acknowledgements

SO MANY PEOPLE have had a part in preparing the material for this book—would that it were possible to list them all by name and thank them individually!

I deeply appreciate the help that has come from my fellow home economists and the other capable technicians who have worked in the various test kitchens to develop and perfect the recipes for this cookbook. I also want to express my gratitude for the generosity of my associates connected with this country's food processors, manufacturers, public relations firms, advertising agencies, associations, and institutions who have given their counsel as well as contributed recipe material and photographs for this book.

A hearty "Thank You" also goes to the foodservice operators who have so willingly submitted time-tested recipes from their busy kitchens.

In addition, very special thanks go to Jule Wilkinson for her valued advice and editing help. And to Charys Pinney, Joan Kocher, and Bridget Janus for their untiring efforts in handling the countless details concerned with publishing.

Eulalia C. Blair

Introduction

THIS BOOK, another member of the series for foodservice menu planning, has to do with garnishes, relishes, and sauces, the important "extras" that "make the difference." It offers recipes for a wide range of accompaniments together with suggestions for decorative touches—a collection to bring excitement, variety, and zest to the meal.

The relish section includes items for the relish tray and for garnishing the plate. There are recipes for colorful, pleasing vegetable relishes, some of them raw, others cooked. And a wondrous family of sweet and/or snappy relishes prepared with fruit. In addition, there is an impressive assortment of piquant jellied relishes designed to complement the entree, add sparkle to the plate.

Recipes for sauces include types that go with entrees, vegetables, and desserts. Cheese sauces, barbecue sauces, flavored butters, and sauces with a tomato base begin a long line of savory sauces that team with entrees. A goodly number of *these dress up meats, poultry, fish, and seafood when presented as hot or as chilled menu items.*

Others in the selection bring out the personality of pasta dishes, omelets, vegetables, and sandwiches of the open type. In addition, there are the different kinds of sweet sauces that give an exciting plus to ice cream, plain cakes, puddings, and other classes of desserts.

Garnishing tips, together with comprehensive lists of suggestions for garnishing soups, entrees, vegetables, salads, and desserts, contribute their share toward completing this book —a book intended to help operators whisk away dullness, entice the eye, and initiate new experiences in dining pleasure.

Garnishes for Sandwiches

Pickle Packers International and Oscar Mayer

GARNISHES

TO GARNISH is to add a pretty touch, to brighten and enliven, to decorate. Yet garnishing should mean more than glamorous looks. In its fullest interpretation a garnish enhances flavor as well as appearance. It is an edible addition that makes good food look better—more inviting. But beyond that, it contrasts and combines with the food it embellishes. It gives rise to an interplay of flavor and textures and adds to eating pleasure.

How do these effective bits of decoration come about? Not by wishful thinking or a magic wand! Spirited garnishing is an art that takes imagination, a certain amount of planning, sensitive fingers, and a deep-down sense of pride.

Good garnishes are the result of an adventurous approach to food presentation. Use imagination when deciding how to cut or arrange them. Let originality come to the fore when thinking up a new garnish to highlight a certain dish.

As guidelines, eight qualifications—color, flavor, texture, shape, size, temperature, spontaneity, and arrangement—help

*keep the garnish in harmony with the character of the dish.
COLOR. Choose colors that brighten the food. A red garnish
outstrips all others for eye-catching effect. But do not under-
estimate the value of the greens and yellows for perk-up tricks.
Color can be brought into play in so many different ways. Try
dipping the tips of lemon wedges in chopped parsley or paprika; sprinkling tomato wedges with basil or chives; rolling
pineapple chunks or orange sections in chopped fresh mint;
nesting a tiny dab of red jelly in a puff of whipped cream or
topping.*

*Use light garnishes on dark foods and the other way around.
Try plump spiced prunes with cold breast of turkey; shiny
black olives with an open crabmeat salad sandwich; a dash of
ground cinnamon on eggnog pie. Similarly, try chopped
hard-cooked egg on a raw spinach leaf salad; halved green
grapes sprinkled through chilled madrilene; a cloverleaf of
blanched whole almonds on a chocolate-iced cookie.*

*Tinting is a simple way to achieve pleasing color effects.
You can give coconut a rainbow of colors—yellow, pink, or
green—by mixing with dry flavored gelatin (1/2 cup gelatin to
a pound of coconut). Tint whipped cream or marshmallow
sauce a delicate shade with food coloring. Try a light pink or
a pale green version to top a mint-flavored chocolate dessert.*

*As another tack, add flavor as well as color by dissolving
red cinnamon candies in the syrup for simmering thick apple
rings or halves of pears. Whatever the approach, do not over-
do it. It is best to limit the usage to a few special items and
always keep the color a delicate shade.*

*FLAVOR. Be sure to choose garnishes to round out and com-
plement flavors. At the same time avoid using too intense
flavors, too pronounced contrasts. Select sweet garnishes for
desserts, piquant garnishes for salads, savory or zesty ones for
entrees. As examples, a small mold of horseradish cream enhances a slice of roast beef; shreds of chipped beef add a new
measure of interest to cream of corn soup; slices of tart pickle
set off a tuna salad; a garnish of cinnamon hard sauce gives a
bonus of taste to a warm apple crisp.*

*Often the most successful garnish for a dish is one that sug-
gests its ingredients. As examples: a whole strawberry atop
a strawberry parfait; a few french fried onion rings beside a
wedge of cheese-and-onion quiche.*

TEXTURE. Take advantage of crisp garnishes as a contrast to soft foods. A few slices of water chestnuts add interest to buttered peas; walnuts add a pleasing crunch to a chocolate cream pie; and crisp croutons do the same thing for a smooth cream of potato soup.

SHAPE. Cut garnishes in neat, evenly shaped pieces. When arranging a display of items, use more than one shape. On a dessert cart, for example, do not have all long garnishes or all round ones. Many items lend themselves to variation through the style of cutting used. To take tomatoes as an illustration, you can cut them crosswise or up-and-down. (Lengthwise slices of Italian tomatoes have an intriguing, "different" look.) You can cut them in petal shape to open for stuffing, or cut wedges (2 thin wedges placed to meet in the center, take the shape of a heart). See picture below.

Fancy shapes cut from pimiento, aspic, truffles, or jellied cranberry sauce make attractive decorations. Small cutters designed for this purpose make this a simple trick. Potato balls, melon balls, radish roses, and corrugated banana slices

Tomato Wedges Arranged for a Heart-Shaped Garnish

American Institute of Baking

are among other pleasing garnishes that, with helpful gadgets, become an easy chore.

SIZE. Keep the size of the garnish in scale with the dish it is garnishing. Remember that the garnish should draw attention to the dish, not become the center of attraction. A well-scaled garnish emphasizes the size of the portion. A topping or sauce used as a garnish should be adequate to accompany the entire serving. A large garnish such as spiced apple rings or a broiled tomato half should relate to the size of the entree on the dinner plate.

TEMPERATURE. Have cold garnishes thoroughly chilled. Be sure that hot garnishes are definitely hot.

Ice has a garnishing role when it imparts a cool, refreshing look to foods that taste best cold. Seafood and fruit cocktails, melon, and all chilled soups are attractive served on a bed of finely chipped ice. Scoops of fruit sherbet take on dazzling picture-book looks when dished up in supreme cups bedded in colored crushed ice in harmonious tones.

One word of warning: always present ice as ice. *It loses its glamor quickly as soon as it starts to melt.*

SPONTANEITY. The most attractive garnishes look fresh, natural, and simple. Avoid over-elaborate garnitures or any

Grapefruit Half Bedded in Colored Ice

Sunkist Growers, Inc.

others that tend to take on a contrived or worked-upon look. A garnish must suggest spontaneity and a certain casualness in order to charm.

Some (but certainly not all) keep their sparkle when prepared a step ahead. You can section grapefruit and oranges; wash small fruits and berries; stuff prunes; make celery sticks and carrot curls. These and many others can be prepared safely in advance. But do not risk fixing any garnish ahead that is apt to lose its bloom.

ARRANGEMENT. Place garnishes to achieve the most artistic effect. The center top may be the most advantageous spot for the garnish. It often is. But some garnishes are more effective arranged in a border or beside the portion, rather than on top of it.

Some garnishes are pleasing when arranged in a pattern, such as crescent-shaped pieces of maraschino cherries arranged as a flower. Slices of cucumber, radish, or pickled beet may be overlapped; slices of canned peaches, sections of mandarin oranges, and similarly shaped pieces of fruit may be grouped as fans, still keeping a pleasing, unaffected look.

The well-chosen, well-placed garnish is sure to set apart the plate it adorns. No garnish looks its prettiest when placed too precisely or when it is plopped down on the dish by a heavy-handed worker who has no aptitude for the garnishing job.

All garnishes need to be arranged with a nimble, lighthanded touch. Some garnishes such as shreds of carrot or green pepper are even at their best dropped from a little distance.

Garnishing Materials

FRESH FRUIT
Strawberries
Other Berries
Grapes
  Halved, seeded
  Small clusters (plain or
    frosted)
Cherries on Stem
Avocado
Plum Slices
Apple
Banana
Pineapple
Kiwi

CITRUS FRUIT
Lemon
  Slices (plain or twisted)
  Wedges
Oranges
  Slices
  Sections
Kumquats
Grapefruit Sections
Lime
  Slices
  Wedges
Grated Orange or Lemon Peel

**CANNED, DRIED, AND
  PRESERVED FRUITS**
Pear
  Halves
  Slices
Peach
  Halves
  Slices
Raisins
Currants
Dates
Figs

Citron
Angelica
Prunes
Preserved Kumquats
Mandarin Orange Sections
Applesauce
Apple
  Chunks
  Slices
  Cinnamon apple rings
Maraschino Cherries
  Red
  Green
Rubyettes

EGGS
Hard-Cooked
  Halves
  Deviled
  Slices
  Wedges
  Sieved
    Yolk
    White
    Whole
Poached

VEGETABLES
Celery
  Hearts
  Curls
  Stuffed bits
Carrot
  Curls
  Sticks
Radish
  Slices
  Roses
Green or Red Pepper
  Rings
  Shreds

Onion
  Slices
  Rings
    (raw or french fried)
  Chopped
  Scallions
  Tiny Pearl
  Red Onion
    Slices
    Rings
Tomato
  Slices
  Wedges
  Cherry tomatoes
    Whole
    Halves
    Stuffed
Cucumber
  Slices (peeled, unpeeled, scored)
  Boats (stuffed)
Asparagus Tips
Beets, Pickled
Fennel
Mushroom
  Slices (raw or cooked)
  Caps (plain or fluted)
  Stuffed
Peas
  (frozen, cooked)
Red Cabbage
  Shreds
Pimiento
  Strips
  Dice
  Cut-outs
Tiny Ears of Corn (canned)
Truffles
Artichoke
  Hearts
  Bottoms
Hearts of Palm

PICKLES, OLIVES
Cucumber Pickles
Mixed Pickles
Mustard Pickles
Pickled or Spiced Fruits
Pickled Walnuts
Pickled Watermelon Rind
Burr Gherkins
Olives
  Ripe
    Whole
    Slices
    Chopped
  Green
    Whole
  Pimiento-stuffed
    Whole
    Slices
Capers

CHEESE
Grated Parmesan
Cheddar or Swiss
  Shredded
  Slices
  Triangles
  Julienne cut
  Cut-outs
  Curls
Cottage
Cream
  Balls (rolled in paprika, nuts, parsley)
  Cubes
  Rosettes

SPICES
Paprika
Nutmeg
Cinnamon
  Ground
  Stick
Whole Cloves

HERBS AND SEEDS
Chives
　Chopped
Parsley
　Sprigs
　Chopped
　Fried
Dill
　Sprigs
Poppy Seed
Sesame Seed
Caraway Seed

LEAVES
Mint
Galax
Chicory
Lemon
Cress
Celery
Grape
Blueberry
Holly

NUTS
Almonds
　Whole (blanched)
　Sliced
　Slivered (plain, sauteed, or
　　toasted)
Brazil Nuts
　Sliced
Coconut
　Fresh
　Shredded
　　Toasted
　　Tinted
　　Chocolate-coated
　Flaked
Filberts
Peanuts

Pecans
　Halves (plain, sugared, glazed,
　　or spiced)
　Chopped
Pistachio
　Chopped
Walnuts
　Halves
　Chopped

SUGAR, CANDY, SYRUPS, JELLY
Cinnamon Candies
Candy Corn
Chocolate Sprinkles
Candied Violets
Sugared Rose Petals
Hard Peppermint Candy
　Whole
　Crushed
Peanut Brittle
　Crushed
Gum Drops
Nonpareils
Lentils
Jordan Almonds
Candied Orange Peel
Candied and Preserved Ginger
Chocolate Curls
Grated Chocolate
Chocolate Designs
Drizzles of Chocolate or Caramel
　Syrup
Confectioners' Sugar
Cinnamon Sugar
Colored Sugar
Jelly
Cranberry Sauce
Flavored Gelatin
　Cubes
　Cut-outs

BREAD, COOKIES, AND
  PASTRY
Croutons
Bread Sticks
Toast
  Triangles
  Circles
  Rings
Rolled Cookies
Wafers
Gaufrettes
Macaroons
Puff Pastry
  Crescents (Fleurons)
  Triangles

MISCELLANEOUS
Anchovy
Shrimp
Sardine
Caviar
  Black
  Red
Bacon Bits
Bacon Curls
Ham Rolls
Salami
  Cornucopias
  Small Sausages
Frankfurter
  Slices
Aspic
  Cut-outs
  Riced
Popcorn
Chinese Noodles
Potato Chips
Whipped Topping
Whipped Cream
  Plain
  Cocoa
  Tinted
  Berry-flavored

Fresh Citrus Garnishes for Eye-Appeal

Sunkist Growers, Inc.

On Garnishing Soups

THE APPEARANCE, eating quality, individuality, and sales value of any soup are influenced by its garnish.

For maximum appearance, soup garnishes should float. Usually they can be sprinkled or dropped on the surface of the soup. The heavier ones are easily managed by laying them on a spoon and slowly lowering into the liquid, It is well worth any extra time and patience it takes for a garnish that enhances the appearance and, at the same time, adds just the right texture and piquancy to individualize the soup.

A choice of garnishes varies the presentation. An accompanying tray, carrying an assortment of a half-dozen garnishes, offered at the table makes something of a ritual of serving soup. As an illustration, thinly sliced pepperoni, tiny sauteed meat balls, shredded green and red pepper, grated parmesan cheese, chopped hard-cooked egg, and herb-flavored croutons might make up the selection for a thick tomato-vegetable soup.

Crouton Garnish for Soup

Kellogg Company

Garnishes for Soups

Cream of Asparagus	Paper-thin slices of Brazil nuts
	Sliced, toasted almonds
	Toasted sesame seed
Bean	Thin frankfurter slices
Bean with Bacon	Add slices of cooked sausage links to the soup; garnish with slices of red apple
Cream of Celery	Paper-thin slice of peeled, fresh tomato
	Crisp Chinese noodles
Cream of Chicken	Grated orange peel
	Curried whipped cream
	Add Madeira; garnish with halved, seeded Ribier grapes
Curried Cream of Chicken	Sauteed flaked coconut
Chicken Gumbo	A scoop of fluffy white rice
Chicken Noodle	Diced pimiento
	Chopped parsley
	Shredded fresh spinach leaves
	Chopped hard-cooked egg
Chicken Rice	Chopped watercress
	Chopped parsley
Clam Chowder	Thin slices of scored, unpeeled cucumber
Consomme	Slices of bamboo shoots
Cream of Leek	Grated, raw carrot
Minestrone	Parmesan cheese
	Tiny meat balls (season ground beef with oregano before shaping)
Cream of Mushroom	Chopped ripe olives
Green Pea	Chopped fresh mint leaves
	Potato-cheese rosettes
	A dollop of sour cream
	Pimiento whipped cream
	Browned whipped cream
Split Pea	A thin, thin slice of red onion
Cream of Potato	Add sherry; garnish with sauteed slivered almonds

Cream of Tomato	A cube of parsley-sprinkled cream cheese
	Salted whipped cream and a sprinkling of sieved egg yolk
	A wisp of fresh dill
Tomato Rice	Crumbled blue cheese
Vegetable	Finely chopped ripe olives
	Chopped parsley and grated parmesan cheese
Cream of Vegetable	A crisp bacon curl

Entree Garnishes

Meat	Bacon, strips or curls
Cheese (for baked casserole items)	Parmesan, grated
	Cheddar, shredded
	Process American, slices, strips, triangles
Olives	Ripe or Pimiento-Stuffed, whole
Pickles	Sliced Cucumber
	Mustard
	Mixed
	Pickled Fruit
	Peaches
	Pears
	Watermelon Rind
	Spiced Prunes
Vegetables	Artichoke Bottoms, stuffed
	Chicory Leaves
	Kabobs of Vegetables
	Mushrooms, stuffed
	Mushroom Caps, whorled and sauteed
	Onion Rings, raw or french fried
	Parsley Sprigs
	Parsley, fried
	Green Pepper Rings
	Tomato Half, broiled
	Spinach-Stuffed Tomato, baked
	Cherry Tomatoes, whole or halves
	Watercress, bouquet

Fruit

Banana, broiled
Cinnamon Apple Rings
Grapes, clusters
Kabobs of Fruit
Kumquats, preserved, whole
Peach Halves, canned, stuffed, and/or
  broiled
Pear Halves, broiled
Pear Halves, stuffed with jelly
Pineapple Slices, broiled

Miscellaneous

Cranberry Sauce or Relish, in lemon
  boat or orange shell
Molded Relishes

Lasagne Mornay Topped with Asparagus Spears

Durum Macaroni HRI Program

On Garnishing Vegetables

GARNISHES ADD DASH—and often a new eating quality— to vegetables that are served singly or in combination. You can draw on vegetables to garnish other vegetables; use mushrooms, for example, and pimiento, white or red onion rings, shreds of green pepper, snipped parsley or chives. A partial list of other likely garnishes includes almonds, croutons, slivered ripe olives, crumbled bacon, and grated cheese, as well as hard-cooked eggs cut in wedges or slices or chopped.

GARNISHES FOR VEGETABLES

For Asparagus	Shredded or grated raw carrot, pimiento strips, or hollandaise sauce
For Cut Green Beans	Green limas, pearl onions, mushrooms, shredded raw carrot, or cauliflowerettes
For Italian Green Beans	Diced pimiento
For Harvard Beets	Thinly sliced kumquats or slivered orange peel
For Broccoli	Sauteed sliced mushrooms or slivered almonds
For Brussels Sprouts	Sliced water chestnuts and red onion rings, sauteed mushrooms, peas, seedless white grapes, chopped walnuts, pearl onions, or cauliflowerettes
For Carrots	Halved and seeded red grapes
For Diagonally-Cut Celery	Sauteed slivered almonds or blanched green pepper shreds
For Cooked Mixed Greens	Lemon wedge, chopped hard-cooked egg, crumbled bacon, or julienne beets
For Corn or Succotash	Diced pimiento, sauteed slivered almonds, or blanched green pepper shreds
For Fordhook Limas	Diced pimiento

For Steamed Halves of Spanish Onions	Sauteed chopped mushrooms, diced pimiento, and chopped parsley
For Peas	Crumbled bacon, slivered ripe olives, sprinkling of chopped dried beef, tiny new potatoes, sliced water chestnuts, shredded raw carrot, or sauteed sliced mushrooms
For Baked (and Slashed) Sweet Potatoes	A spoonful of orange marmalade
For Candied Sweet Potatoes	Coarsely chopped walnuts, pineapple tidbits, or orange slices
For Mashed Sweet Potatoes or Winter Squash	Sauteed slivered almonds or toasted sesame seeds
For Halves or Rings of Acorn Squash	Peas, pearl onions, or halved brussels sprouts
For Spinach	Wedge of lemon, crumbled bacon, or a slice or wedge of hard-cooked egg
For Stewed Tomatoes	Garlic croutons
For Stewed Tomatoes with Eggplant	White onion rings

Salad Garnishes

FOR GREEN SALADS

Meat	Crisp bacon, crumbled
	Ham, chicken, or tongue, cut julienne
Fish	Anchovy fillets
	Sardines
Eggs	Hard-cooked, wedges, slices
Cheese	Cheddar, grated or cubes
	Swiss, cut julienne
	Parmesan, grated
Olives	Green, pimiento-stuffed, slices
	Ripe olives, pitted

(continued)

Vegetable Salad with Anchovy Garnish

American Dairy Association

Vegetables	Artichoke hearts
	Red cabbage, shreds
	Cauliflower, raw, slices, or cauliflow-erettes
	Cucumber, slices
	Mushrooms, raw slices
	Red onion, rings
	Hearts of palm
	Pimiento, strips
	Radish, slices
	Tomato, wedges or slices
	Cherry tomatoes, whole or halves
	Zucchini, raw, slices
Fruit	Avocado, slices or chunks
	Orange or grapefruit, sections
	Pomegranate seeds
Miscellaneous	Croutons, herbed, cheese, or plain
	Water chestnuts, sliced

FOR VEGETABLE SALADS

Meat	Liver sausage, balls rolled in chopped parsley
Eggs	Hard-cooked, slices, wedges, or halves (plain or deviled)
	Hard-cooked, slice, topped with chopped parsley
Olives	Green, ripe, pimiento-stuffed, whole
Vegetables	Artichoke hearts
	Pickled beets, slices or julienne strips
	Carrot, raw, grated
	Chives, chopped
	Hearts of palm
	Parsley, sprigs or chopped
	Green pepper, shreds or rings
	Pimiento, strips
	Radishes
	Scallions, whole
	Tomatoes, wedges or slices
	Cherry tomatoes, whole
	Italian tomatoes, lengthwise slices
	Watercress, sprigs

FOR FRUIT SALADS

Fruits	Avocado, sliced or diced
	Banana, scored and cut diagonally
	Banana chunks, coated with mayonnaise and rolled in chopped nuts
	Scattering of blueberries, blackberries, or raspberries
	Whole strawberries with bright green caps
	Maraschino cherries, red or green
	Ripe sweet cherries on stem
	Grapes, Ribier, halves, seeded, and sandwiched with cream cheese
	Grapes, seedless, small cluster
	Kiwi, peeled, sliced
	Kumquat, fresh or preserved, thinly sliced

(continued)

Fruits (cont.)	Lemon or lime, wedges
	Orange, wedges
	Pineapple chunks, rolled in chopped, fresh mint leaves
	Plums, fresh, sliced, and lightly sweetened
	Prunes, stuffed with cheese or nuts
	Raisins, plumped
Miscellaneous	Cheese and nut balls
	Coconut, flaked
	Ginger, candied or preserved, chopped
	Mint, sprigs, plain or dusted with confectioners' sugar
	Orange peel, candied, chopped
	Sherbet, small scoop
	Watercress, sprigs

FOR CHICKEN OR SEAFOOD SALADS

Eggs	Hard-cooked, slices or wedges
Cheese	Cheddar or Swiss, shredded
Olives	Green, ripe, pimiento-stuffed, whole
Pickles	Capers
	Burr gherkins
	Cucumber pickles
	Spiced peach, pear, watermelon rind
Nuts	Almonds, slivered, toasted
	Salted pecan halves
Fruit	Avocado, rings, slices, or halves
	Cranberry sauce, jellied or whole
	Seedless grapes, small cluster
	Kabobs of pineapple chunks, avocado cubes
	Kumquats, preserved, whole
	Lemon, wedges (for seafood)
Vegetables	Asparagus tips
	Parsley, sprigs
	Pimiento, strips
	Radishes
	Cherry tomatoes, whole or halves
	Tomato wedges, dipped in chopped chives
	Watercress, sprigs
Miscellaneous	Candied ginger, small bits
	Paprika

Aspics

BASIC CLEAR ASPIC

Yield: 1 gallon

Ingredients

GELATINE, UNFLAVORED	2-1/4 ounces
STOCK, well-seasoned (clear, fat-free)	1 gallon

Procedure

1. Sprinkle gelatine on stock. Heat and stir until gelatine is dissolved.
2. Chill until of syrupy consistency. Use as a glaze or for lining molds, and/or chill until firm and cut aspic into cubes or force through ricer to garnish displays of aspic-glazed poached fish or of jellied meat, poultry, or fish items prepared in molds.

GOURMET GELATINE GLAZE

Yield: 2 quarts

Ingredients

WATER	1-3/4 quarts
SUGAR	1/3 cup
SEASONED SALT	1-1/2 teaspoons
ONION SALT	1 tablespoon
SALT	1-1/2 teaspoons
WHITE PEPPER	1/8 teaspoon
GELATINE, UNFLAVORED	1-1/2 ounces
LEMON JUICE	1-1/2 cups

Procedure

1. Combine water with sugar, seasonings, and gelatine; bring to a boil, stirring until gelatine is dissolved. Add lemon juice; strain through cheesecloth.
2. Cool until mixture begins to thicken. Spoon over meat or other cold food to be glazed; refrigerate until set.
3. Spoon on another layer of the slightly thickened glaze; chill until set. Use over ham, fish, meat, poultry, game, eggs, jellied loaves, or molds.

CHAUD-FROID GLAZE*

Yield: 1-1/3 quarts

Ingredients

ROUX	4 ounces
CHICKEN BROTH	1 quart
GELATINE, UNFLAVORED	1 ounce
WATER, cold	1 cup
EGG YOLKS	2
CREAM, HEAVY	1/2 cup

Procedure

1. Stir roux into broth; cook and stir until mixture thickens and comes to a boil. Cook over very low heat for 5 minutes.

2. Soften gelatine in cold water. Stir into hot mixture until dissolved.

3. Beat egg yolks with cream; blend with sauce. Heat and stir 2 minutes. *Do not boil.*

4. Remove from heat. Chill until mixture thickens sufficiently to adhere to meat and give a smooth, even glaze. (If glaze becomes too thick and forms thick patches on meat, heat slightly to regain proper consistency.)

*A jellied white coating for meats, poultry, or items prepared in molds for buffet service. Dishes are usually completed with cut-out garnishes of pimiento, truffles, etc.

TOMATO ASPIC

Yield: 42 3-ounce portions

Ingredients

TOMATO JUICE	3 quarts
SUGAR	1/4 cup
SALT	1 tablespoon
ONION, chopped	1/2 cup
CELERY LEAVES	2 cups
BAY LEAVES, SMALL	2
CLOVES, WHOLE	1/2 teaspoon
WHOLE BLACK PEPPER	1/4 teaspoon
GELATINE, UNFLAVORED	1/2 cup (2-1/2 ounces)
TOMATO JUICE	1 quart
LEMON JUICE	3/4 cup

Procedure

1. Combine first amount of tomato juice, sugar, salt, onion, celery leaves, bay leaves, cloves, and whole black pepper. Cover; simmer 15 minutes.

2. Soften gelatine in second amount of tomato juice.

3. Strain hot tomato mixture; add to softened gelatine; stir until dissolved. Add lemon juice.

4. Turn into small individual molds or shallow pans. Chill until firm.

5. Unmold or cut into squares. Arrange on crisp greens, if desired. Use to garnish hot or cold fish dishes, cold plates, salads, etc.

HOW TO PORTION CANNED JELLIED CRANBERRY SAUCE

To Cut 4-Ounce Portions From No. 10 Can.
1. Punch hole in bottom of can.
2. Remove top.
3. Slide complete mold from can.
4. Cut mold in half lengthwise.
5. Cut each half lengthwise into thirds.
6. Cut 1-inch wedges.

  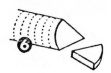

Pack	Portion Yield	
No. 10 Jellied	29—4 oz.	58—2 oz.
No. 300 Jellied	4—4 oz.	8—2 oz.
No. 10 Whole	29—4 oz.	58—2 oz.
No. 300 Whole	4—4 oz.	8—2 oz.

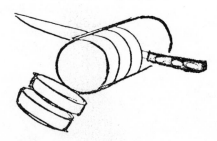

How to Slice No. 200 Can Giving Round Slices

Fruit Garnishes

ORANGE CUPS FILLED WITH CINNAMON FRUIT SALAD

Yield: 25 portions

Ingredients

SOUR CREAM	2 cups
ORANGE PEEL, freshly grated	2 tablespoons
ORANGE JUICE, freshly squeezed	3 tablespoons
HONEY	1-1/2 tablespoons
CINNAMON	1-1/4 teaspoons
ORANGES, MEDIUM-SIZED or SMALL	25
MIXED FRUITS FOR SALAD, drained	1 No. 10 can
MINT SPRIGS	25

Procedure

1. Combine sour cream, orange peel, orange juice, honey, and cinnamon. Mix well. Refrigerate at least 1 hour to blend flavors.

2. Cut tops from oranges. Scoop out fruit, taking care to keep orange peel cups intact. Cut fruit into bite-sized pieces and add to drained mixed fruits.

3. Add sour cream mixture to fruit. Toss lightly until well combined.

4. Pile fruit into orange cups. Garnish with fresh mint sprigs.

FRUIT PUFF MEAT GARNISH

Yield: 50 garnishes

Ingredients

MAYONNAISE	3 cups
SWEET PICKLES, chopped	1/2 cup
PEACH or PEAR HALVES, CANNED	50

Procedure

1. Mix mayonnaise and pickles.

2. Pile mixture on halves of fruit. Broil until filling puffs and browns. Serve hot.

PEARS SUPREME

Yield: approximately 25 portions

Ingredients

PEAR HALVES	1 No. 10 can
HONEY	1 cup
SOUR CREAM	2 cups
WALNUTS, coarsely chopped	2 cups

Procedure

1. Drain pears well.

2. Combine honey and sour cream.

3. Coat pear halves with mixture. Arrange in buttered broiler pan, cut-side down.

4. Broil until sauce bubbles. Turn carefully; baste; cover cut-side of pears with chopped walnuts. Continue broiling until walnuts are slightly toasted.

5. Serve warm as a garnish for turkey, chicken, or ham.

CINNAMON PEARS

Yield: 40 to 50 garnishes

Ingredients

PEAR HALVES	1 No. 10 can
CLOVES, WHOLE	as needed
PEAR SYRUP and WATER to equal	1-1/2 quarts
VINEGAR	1 cup
SUGAR	3 cups
CINNAMON STICKS, 3-inch	3
RED FOOD COLORING (optional)	as needed

Procedure

1. Drain pears, reserving syrup.

2. Stud each pear half with 2 or 3 cloves; refrigerate overnight.

3. Next day, add water to reserved pear syrup to make required amount. Add vinegar, sugar, and cinnamon sticks. Simmer 10 to 12 minutes. Cool.

4. Remove cinnamon sticks. Add red coloring, if desired. Pour syrup over pears. Chill overnight to allow fruit to develop flavor and take on color (if used). Use as a garnish for grilled cheese sandwiches or platters of sliced cold turkey or other meats.

Vegetable Garnishes

POTATO-CHEESE ROSETTES
(See picture below)

Yield: 50 garnishes

Ingredients

INSTANT MASHED POTATOES	12 ounces
WATER, boiling	3 cups
SALT	1-1/2 teaspoons
BUTTER or MARGARINE	2 ounces
MILK, hot	2 cups
EGG YOLKS	4
CHEESE, PARMESAN or CHEDDAR, grated	6 ounces

Procedure

1. Prepare mashed potatoes according to label directions, using above proportions of water, salt, butter, and hot milk.

2. Add egg yolks, one at a time, beating to blend.

3. Force through pastry tube onto greased baking sheet making small rosettes or rings. Top with cheese.

4. Brown lightly in oven at 425°F.

Potato-Cheese Rosettes (Recipe, above)

Idaho-Oregon Promotion Committee

FLUTING MUSHROOMS

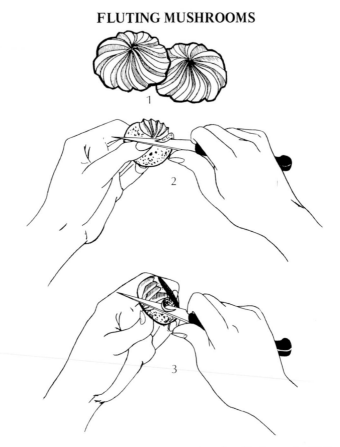

American Mushroom Institute

Directions:
1. Fluted mushrooms make an attractive and delicious garnish.
2. To flute a mushroom, hold a small sharp paring knife motionless in your right hand, with the cutting edge turned away from your body. Wrap your fingers around the handle of the knife and steady the mushroom cap with the thumb of your right hand. Select a spot about halfway down the knife blade as the cutting edge.
3. Holding the knife in your right hand motionless, bring the crown—the very middle—of the mushroom to the knife edge. Press very lightly against mushroom skin, turning the cap as you cut away a very thin strip of skin. If you have turned the mushroom cap correctly, you will have cut a swirling, very shallow groove. Repeat these cuts, spacing them evenly around the mushroom.

Dessert Garnishes

Sunkist Growers, Inc.

Fresh Fruit

Avocado slices
Apple, unpeeled red slices
Banana slices
Blueberries
Cherries, sweet, on stem
Cranberries, glazed
Grapes
  Halves, seeded
  Clusters, plain or sugared
Kiwi, peeled slices
Kumquat, thin slices
Lemon
  Slices, plain or twisted
  Wedges
  Grated peel
Lime
  Slices, plain or twisted
  Wedges
Melon balls, cantaloupe, honeydew,
  watermelon
Orange
  Slices
  Sections
  Grated peel
Pineapple
  Cubes
  Fans
Plums, slices
Raspberries
Strawberries
  Whole, plain or with caps
  Slices

Canned, Dried, and
Preserved Fruit

Apricots
  Halves
  Slices
Angelica
Currants
Maraschino cherries
  Red, whole, sliced, chopped, on stem
  Green, whole, sliced, chopped, on stem
Citron

Dates
  Slices
  Strips
  Stuffed with nuts or hard sauce
Figs, strips
Kumquats
  Whole
  Slices
Mandarin orange sections
Pears, plain or tinted
  Halves
  Slices
Peaches
  Halves
  Slices
Prunes, seeded halves
Raisins

Nuts

Almonds
  Blanched whole, plain, or end dipped
    in chocolate
  Sliced
  Slivered (plain or toasted)
Brazil nuts, slices
Coconut
  Fresh
  Shredded
    Toasted
    Tinted
    Chocolate-coated
  Flaked
Filberts, whole
Peanuts
  Whole
  Chopped
Pecans
  Halves, plain, sugared, glazed, or
    spiced
  Chopped
Pistachio, chopped
Walnuts
  Halves
  Chopped

Sugar, Candy, Syrups, Jelly	Confectioners' sugar
	Cinnamon sugar
	Colored sugar
	Candy corn
	Candied orange peel
	Candied and preserved ginger
	Cinnamon candies
	Gum drops
	Hard peppermint candy
	Whole
	Crushed
	Peanut brittle, crushed
	Lentils
	Nonpareils
	Jordan almonds
	Chocolate mint patties
	Chocolate sprinkles
	Chocolate curls
	Grated chocolate
	Chocolate designs
	Drizzles of chocolate or caramel syrup
	Cranberry sauce
	Flavored gelatin
	Cubes
	Cut-outs
	Jelly
Cookies	Gaufrettes
	Macaroons
	Rolled cookies
	Wafers
Spice	Cinnamon
	Nutmeg
Miscellaneous	Hard sauce balls or cut-outs
	Whipped cream
	Plain, flavored
	Cocoa
	Tinted
	Berry-flavored
	Whipped topping

Beverage Garnishes

Sunkist Growers, Inc.

HOW TO MAKE ATTRACTIVE CITRUS GARNISHES

BASIC CARTWHEELS
With a French knife, cut slices of the fruit crosswise to the desired thickness. Grapefruit, oranges, lemons, and limes are used for cartwheels. The fruit sectioner is excellent for cutting orange and lemon cartwheels. They can be cut ahead of need and stored in large sealed glass containers or plastic bags without loss of moisture or beauty.

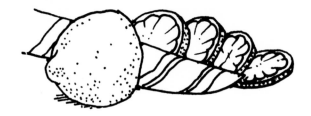

CESTEURED EDGE CARTWHEELS
1. Hold stem end and blossom end of fruit with thumb and middle finger.
2. Cesteur peel from end to end leaving about 1/4 to 1/2 inch between each cut.
3. Cut cartwheels to desired thickness.

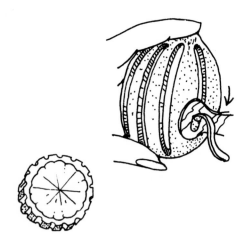

Sunkist Growers, Inc.

DECORATED CARTWHEELS:
Use any one of the following to decorate plain or cesteured cartwheels:

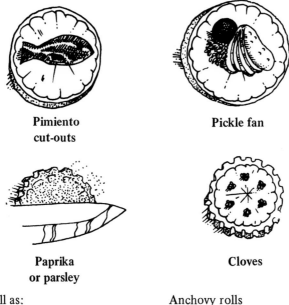

Pimiento   Pickle fan
cut-outs

Paprika   Cloves
or parsley

As well as: Anchovy rolls
Broccoli flowerets   Cherries
Sculptured mushrooms   Mint leaves

SCALLOPED BORDER FOR TRAYS, PLATTERS
OR CARVING BOARDS

1. Place half-cartwheels of orange or grapefruit on outer edge of tray to be garnished end to end.
2. Place second layer of smaller half-cartwheels (lemon) on top of first layer, aligning cut edge.
3. Place third layer of still smaller half-cartwheels (lime) last. A scalloped, layered effect results.

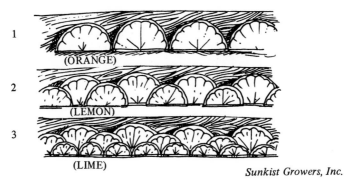

1   (ORANGE)

2   (LEMON)

3   (LIME)

Sunkist Growers, Inc.

CARTWHEEL TWISTS:
1. Use plain or cesteured cartwheel.
2. Make one cut into cartwheel from edge of peel to center.
3. Twist ends in opposite directions, standing cartwheel gently.
4. Use plain or decorate with cherry, parsley, or watercress.

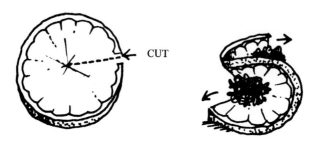

CARTWHEEL TWIST BORDER:
1. Use cartwheel twists to make a continuous border around platter or tray.
2. Place first cartwheel twist and secure with wooden pick.
3. Continue counterclockwise to build border.
4. Slip right end of cartwheel under first cartwheel, leaving left end exposed.
5. Border can be accented with green and red maraschino cherries.

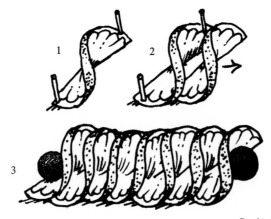

Sunkist Growers, Inc.

STAR GARNISH:
1. Hold fruit with thumb and middle finger at stem and blossom ends.
2. Make a "jaws" sawtooth-cut around middle, cutting to inside center of fruit. Cut through each time to allow clean separation.
3. Using both hands, gently pull fruit apart. If it does not pull apart, cut through skin still uncut. Then separate.

Sunkist Growers, Inc.

CHRYSANTHEMUM FLOWER:

1. Use star-cut method, making "jaws" sawtooth-cut longer, cutting teeth from within 3/4 inch of blossom end and stem end.
2. Separate.
3. Remove "meat" from petals with fingers, saving "meat" for use in fruit cup. Be sure peel is clean.
4. Use grapefruit, orange, lemon, and lime.
5. With a pointed wooden skewer, place two grapefruit flowers on skewer, then two orange flowers, then lemon and last lime.
6. Cut wooden skewer "stem" of flower to length needed. If flower is not to be used right away, place in plastic to keep fresh.
7. Surround flower with watercress or other greens.

STAR CUPS:

1. Use an orange or grapefruit.
2. Make sawtooth-cut finer and not as deep as for the chrysanthemum flowers.

Sunkist Growers, Inc.

3. Using a grapefruit knife, clean out "meat," leaving enough "meat" next to peel for color.

4. Fill cups with berries, sherbet, puddings, relishes, etc.

BEVERAGE GARNISHES:

TIKI SAILS: Use an orange, lemon, and lime cartwheel and skewer. Thread the orange first onto the skewer through the peel, the lemon next, and the lime last.

KABOBS: 1. Cut cartwheel into quarters. Thread two quarters onto wooden pick, placing a cherry between each. 2. and 3. Use either lemon or orange twists to thread onto wooden pick, along with olive, cherry, or onion. 4. Cut off the end of an orange or lemon that has been cesteured diagonally. Place on end of skewer with cherry.

Sunkist Growers, Inc.

CITRUS ROSES:

Roses can be made from grapefruit, oranges, lemons, and tangerines. Western-grown grapefruit have slightly thicker peel, letting you make two roses from one fruit. After cutting off thin outer peel, cut inner white membrane.

1. Peel the outer colored skin in a wide, thin, continuous spiral.
2. Place the peel in near-boiling water for one or two minutes to make it more flexible. Cool with cold water to handle easily.
3. To make rose, wind peel in reverse, colored side in with white side out.
4. Starting with the center of the rose, form the peel tightly into a bud. Secure with wooden pick at base.
5. Continue forming flower by keeping petals next to stem tight, letting outer part be looser. Secure flower at base with wooden pick as rose is formed.
6. Place in ice water to set flower.
7. Cut off visible part of wooden picks before placing in arrangement.

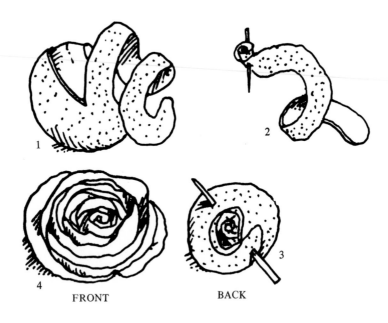

FRONT   BACK

Sunkist Growers, Inc.

CITRUS PEEL FLOWERS:

Flowers can be made from the reamed-out shells of grapefruit, oranges, lemons, tangerines, and limes.

1. Cut fruit in half and ream juice.
2. Remove fiber from shells.
3. Using shears or paring knife, cut from outer edge to within 1/2 inch of center, making six petals.
4. Petals can be left as cut or can be rounded or made pointed.
5. Place a colored cherry or olive in center of each flower.
6. Flowers can be made ahead of usage. Place flat between wet towelling.
7. Combine with seasonal greenery or place on bed of ice (for cafeterias).

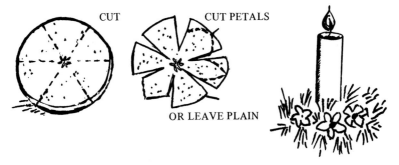

CUT   CUT PETALS

OR LEAVE PLAIN

LEMON NAPKIN RINGS:

For special intimate parties, surprise customers with lemon napkin rings.

1. Cut lemon in half and ream juice (use in punch or at bar).
2. Clean out fiber.
3. Cut each half into two slices, so that each lemon makes four circles. These napkin rings fit easily around large paper or linen napkins. Finish each with a sprig of seasonal greenery. Add a bright cherry or cranberry.

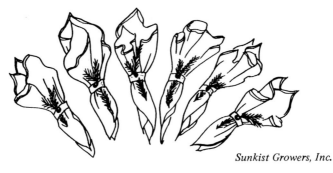

Sunkist Growers, Inc.

Relishes for Open-Faced Sandwich

National Sandwich Idea Contest

RELISHES

IT IS EASY to see how relishes received their name. In common usage, "to relish" means to enjoy. What, then, could be more natural than to apply the term relishes *to that wide range of accompaniments that bring excitement, variety, flavor, and zest to a meal?*

When the umbrella that covers relishes is opened wide, it spans a tremendous variety and a number of different types. Crisp raw vegetables make up one of the major groupings. Olives and pickles comprise another of similar importance.

In addition, there are various and sundry chopped vegetable mixtures, some of them raw, others cooked. Then consider the wondrous family of relishes prepared with fruit. This includes spiced fruits and tart fruit sauces, along with a number of fruit butters, jellies, and preserves, as well as ices and sherbets when served as an adjunct to poultry or meat.

Certain condiments rise to relish stature, as do gelatin creations that are definitely of a piquant nature. Salted nuts comprise another but smaller section. Cottage cheese, plain or tossed with vegetables, shapes still another type of relish.

Raw vegetables, well chilled and crisp, present a treasure trove of possibilities for colorful, pleasing, and lively *relishes. Even a limited selection of two or three vegetables, with or without olives, adds a gala touch to a meal if their freshness is at its prime and an element of drama is woven in. To come off successfully, the vegetables must be scrupulously clean, bright, perky, and brittle-crisp. Presenting them with a tasty dip ushers in a nice surprise.*

But this is only one of several ways to lift a simple relish offering above the routine. Introducing a seldom-met-up-with item will turn the trick. So will well-planned assortments that display striking contrasts in color and an intriguing variety of shapes. Effective, too, are serving dishes that reach beyond the conventional, especially when utilized to work out imaginative, eye-catching arrangements.

The long list of vegetables from which to choose offers a splendid opportunity to create excitement with items that are not usually identified as relishes, to say nothing of the recipe-made specialties that can arouse interest and make the desired impact as piquant accompaniments.

Cherry tomatoes, raw turnip or zucchini sticks, marinated sliced mushrooms or cauliflowerettes, celery root, or spinach salad mixtures can breathe new life into a relish offering. Celery, carrots, and radishes, the genial standbys, escape the trite by appearing in a different shape. Try offering stuffed celery, celery sticks, or quartered hearts; shredded carrots, carrot curls, crinkle-cut sticks, and long diagonal slices; radish roses, radish fans, and white icicle radishes in slender strips.

The popular tomato gains a new response when it appears in new styles. Experiment with tomato wedges with a sprinkling of snipped fresh basil, tomato slices with strips of avocado and chopped parsley, and lengthwise slices of Italian tomatoes.

When fashioning a relish selection, be sure to feature a variety of shapes. Avoid having everything round, or chopped, or cut in strips.

Serving equipment provides another approach for bringing relishes to the fore. For an exciting newness, experiment with square, rectangular, or leaf-shaped relish dishes. Or, try making the presentation in a pretty wooden, glass, or chinaware bowl. A lazy-susan arrangement can work on a show-

piece scale when a wide selection of relishes is to be left on the table. Trays that come fitted with rows of identical inserts function successfully for assembling impressive assortments to be passed from table to table or, for a buffet. Other equipment having 3 or 4 wells works out nicely for a more modest selection of relishes to be passed. Individual portions, served direct from the kitchen, can be contained in paper souffle dishes or small lettuce cups.

Ripe, green, and stuffed olives come ready to serve as do pickles of almost every description. Small cucumber pickles, dill pickle spears, and the like keep good company with vegetables and olives in a relish dish. Pickle chips, mustard pickles, corn relish, pickled beets, chopped cabbage relishes, cooked eggplant mixtures, and similar items are best each kept to its own separate dish.

The same rule applies to many of the fruit relishes, condiments, cottage cheese, and nuts. Whole fruits such as preserved kumquats and the spiced fruits which include peaches, prunes, crabapples, and pears, are seldom free from a bit of their syrup. Applesauce, whole cranberry sauce, raw cranberry relish, apple butter, and jelly illustrate other fruit relishes that, like chutney, chili sauce, and other condiments, quite obviously, require dishes of their own.

Pieces of hot broiled fruits (peach or pear halves, pineapple slices, and such), sauteed bananas, and curried fruits are usually served directly on the dinner plate. While actually a relish, they double as garnish. Relish items prepared with gelatin likewise perform this dual function.

When planning an assortment of relishes, it is well to give thought to items that complement the entree features. By way of suggestion: include a Cucumber Relish Mold for fish; Applesauce Pimiento Relish for pork; a Jellied Horseradish Cream for roast beef; Corn Relish for chopped sirloin; Cranberry Orange Relish for poultry; Spiced Prunes for roast veal; Molded Mustard Relish for corned beef, and Mango Chutney for a menu starring a curry of lamb.

Fruit Relishes

CRANBERRY-RICE RELISH

Yield: 36 1/4-cup portions

Ingredients

RICE, cooked	1-1/2 cups
SAUTERNE	2/3 cup
CRANBERRIES, FRESH	1 quart
ORANGES, quartered, seeded	2
SUGAR	1 cup
MINCEMEAT, BRANDY-FLAVORED	1 cup
PECANS, broken	1 cup

Procedure

1. Marinate rice in sauterne for 3 hours.
2. Grind cranberries and oranges. Add sugar, mincemeat, and nuts. Let chill while rice marinates.
3. Combine cranberry mixture and rice.

FRESH CRANBERRY APPLE-BIT RELISH

Yield: 6-1/2 quarts

Ingredients

CRANBERRIES	6 pounds
RAISINS, SEEDLESS	1 pound
APPLE SLICES	1 No. 10 can
WALNUTS, chopped	3 cups
SUGAR	3 pounds
LEMON JUICE	2 tablespoons

Procedure

1. Chop cranberries and raisins coarsely.
2. Dice apples; combine with cranberry mixture. Add walnuts; sugar, and lemon juice; mix well.
3. Chill in refrigerator for several hours before serving.

CRANBERRY-ORANGE RELISH

Yield: 50 portions

Ingredients

CRANBERRIES, FRESH	3 pounds
ORANGES, quartered, seeded	6
SUGAR	3 pounds

Procedure

1. Wash and sort cranberries.
2. Put cranberries and oranges through grinder. Add sugar; mix well. Chill.

Note

This relish will keep, refrigerated, for several weeks. Or, it may be frozen for future use, if desired.

CRANBERRY-WALNUT RELISH

Yield: 1 quart

Ingredients

WALNUT MEATS, coarsely broken	1 cup
WHOLE-CRANBERRY SAUCE	2 1-pound cans
ORANGE MARMALADE	1 cup
LEMON JUICE	1 tablespoon

Procedure

1. Spread walnuts in shallow pan. Toast in oven at 350°F. until light golden brown, about 12 minutes.
2. Combine toasted walnuts, cranberry sauce, orange marmalade, and lemon juice. Chill.

HORSERADISH CRANBERRY CREAM

Yield: approximately 1-1/4 quarts

Ingredients

WHOLE-CRANBERRY SAUCE	2 1-pound cans
SOUR CREAM	2 cups
FRESH or FROZEN HORSERADISH	6 tablespoons
LEMON JUICE	2 tablespoons

Procedure

Combine ingredients; chill. Serve with fried or broiled fish.

MANGO CHUTNEY

Yield: 1 gallon

Ingredients

SUGAR, LIGHT BROWN	4 pounds
RAISINS, SEEDLESS	3 cups
CIDER VINEGAR	3 cups
SALT	1 teaspoon
GARLIC POWDER	1/2 teaspoon
GINGER, GROUND	2-1/2 tablespoons
DRIED HOT RED PEPPERS, crumbled	2
MANGOS, UNDER-RIPE, cubed	1 gallon (10 large)
GREEN PEPPER, chopped	2 cups
TOMATOES, MEDIUM-SIZED, RIPE, chopped	4
ONION, diced	1 cup

Procedure

1. Combine brown sugar, raisins, vinegar, salt, garlic powder, ginger, and red peppers in a 12-quart kettle. Heat, stirring, until sugar is dissolved.

2. Add remaining ingredients. Cook over medium-low heat until thick, 2 to 3 hours, stirring occasionally.

3. Pour into hot sterilized jars. Seal at once. Serve with curried dishes.

ORANGE-CRANBERRY CHUTNEY ⟶

Yield: 1-1/4 quarts

Ingredients

ORANGES	4
ORANGE PEEL, slivered	1/4 cup
ORANGE JUICE	1/2 cup
WORCESTERSHIRE SAUCE	1 tablespoon
GARLIC, peeled	1 clove
LIQUID HOT PEPPER SEASONING	1/2 teaspoon
SUGAR	2 cups
RAISINS	1/2 cup
CURRY POWDER	2 teaspoons
CRYSTALLIZED GINGER, diced	1/2 cup
CINNAMON STICK	1
CRANBERRIES	1 pound

APPLE CHUTNEY

Yield: 2-1/4 quarts

Ingredients

APPLE SLICES, CANNED	6-1/4 cups (3 pounds)
SUGAR, LIGHT BROWN	2-1/2 cups
CIDER VINEGAR	2/3 cup
CANDIED GINGER, slivered	1-1/4 cups (8 ounces)
ONION, thinly sliced	1-1/4 cups (6 ounces)
RAISINS, WHITE, SEEDLESS	2-1/2 cups (1 pound)
CHILI POWDER	2-1/2 teaspoons (1 ounce)
SALT	1-1/4 teaspoons
MUSTARD SEED	5 teaspoons (1 ounce)
PIMIENTO, diced	1-1/4 cups (10 ounces)
WALNUTS, chopped	1-1/4 cups (5 ounces)

Procedure

1. Chop apple slices. Combine with brown sugar, vinegar, ginger, onion, raisins, chili powder, salt, and mustard seed. Bring to a boil; simmer 30 minutes.

2. Add pimiento and walnuts. Chill.

Procedure

1. Peel oranges with paring knife, removing all white membrane. Slice 1/4 inch thick; cut slices in half.

2. Combine orange peel, orange juice, Worcestershire sauce, garlic, liquid hot pepper seasoning, sugar, raisins, curry powder, ginger, cinnamon, and cranberries. Cook, stirring, over medium heat until sugar dissolves. Continue cooking until cranberries pop, about 10 minutes.

3. Remove garlic clove and cinnamon stick. Stir in sliced oranges; heat until mixture comes to a boil. To store, pour into hot sterilized jars; seal at once with paraffin.

4. Serve hot or cold with poultry, ham, or roast pork.

CHERRY CHUTNEY

Yield: 1 gallon

Ingredients

CHERRIES, RED, SOUR, PITTED (WATER PACK)	1 No. 10 can
CHERRY JUICE and WATER to equal	7-1/2 cups
SUGAR	1-1/2 pounds
CORNSTARCH	2-1/2 ounces
SALT	2 teaspoons
DRY MUSTARD	1 tablespoon
GINGER, GROUND	1 teaspoon
RAISINS	2 cups
PICKLING SPICE	3 tablespoons
LEMON JUICE	2/3 cup
RED FOOD COLORING (optional)	1 teaspoon

Procedure

1. Drain cherries; measure juice. Add water to make required amount.

2. Mix sugar, cornstarch, salt, mustard, and ginger. Stir in liquid. Add raisins. Tie pickling spice loosely in cheesecloth. Add to mixture.

3. Cook, stirring, until mixture comes to a boil. Boil for 1 minute.

4. Remove from heat. Remove spice bag. Add drained cherries, lemon juice, and if desired, the red food coloring. Heat to boiling. Serve hot or cold.

HOT CHILI PEACHES

Yield: 32 portions

Ingredients

CLING PEACHES, SLICED	1 No. 10 can
PEACH SYRUP	2 cups
CHILI SAUCE	2 cups
LEMON JUICE	3 tablespoons
WORCESTERSHIRE SAUCE	2 tablespoons
CHILI POWDER	1 teaspoon

Procedure

1. Drain peach slices, reserving required amount of syrup.

2. Combine syrup and seasonings; heat. Add peaches; heat through.

3. Serve with or over hamburgers.

PEACHES WITH HORSERADISH CREAM

Yield: 24 portions

Ingredients

CLING PEACH HALVES, CANNED	48
CREAM, WHIPPING	2 cups
PREPARED HORSERADISH, drained	1/4 cup
SALT	1 teaspoon
VINEGAR	2 teaspoons

Procedure

    1. Chill peach halves. Drain well.

    2. Whip cream until stiff. Fold in horseradish, salt, and vinegar. Spoon into peach halves.

    3. Serve as an accompaniment to cold cuts.

Cling Peach Advisory Board

Hot Peach Garnishes

Pimiento roses are an accompaniment for seafood; steak sauce for beef; chopped canned green chilies and parsley for pork; and pitted prunes stuffed with pickled onion for poultry.

PEACHY PICKLE

Yield: 25 portions

Ingredients

PEACH HALVES	1 No. 10 can
PEACH SYRUP	2 cups
HONEY	1-2/3 cups
ORANGE JUICE	1 cup
WHITE WINE VINEGAR	1 cup
ORANGE PEEL, coarsely grated	1 tablespoon
CLOVES, WHOLE	1 tablespoon

Procedure

1. Drain peaches, reserving required amount of syrup.

2. Combine peach syrup, honey, orange juice, vinegar, orange peel, and cloves. Heat and stir until mixture boils. Boil gently 10 minutes.

3. Add well-drained fruit. Return to boiling; boil gently 5 minutes.

4. Remove from heat. Let fruit stand in syrup overnight before serving.

SPICED PRUNES

Yield: approximately 50 portions

Ingredients

PRUNES, LARGE	6 pounds
WATER, cold	as needed
PRUNE JUICE, from cooking prunes	1-1/2 quarts
VINEGAR	1-1/2 quarts
SUGAR	1-1/2 quarts
CLOVES, GROUND	2 tablespoons
CINNAMON	2 tablespoons

Procedure

1. Rinse prunes; cover with cold water; boil 10 to 12 minutes; drain, reserving juice.

2. Measure prune juice; add water, if necessary, to make required amount. Add vinegar, sugar, and spices; boil 1 minute.

3. Add prunes; bring to a boil. Cool; refrigerate. Let stand at least overnight, several days if possible, to allow flavor to permeate prunes. Serve with pork, veal, or poultry.

PICKLED PRUNES

Yield: approximately 4-1/2 quarts

Ingredients

SUGAR, BROWN	2 pounds
WATER	2 quarts
CIDER VINEGAR	1 quart
PRUNES	5 pounds
CINNAMON, GROUND	1 tablespoon
PICKLING SPICE	2 tablespoons
ONION RINGS (optional)	2 pounds

Procedure

1. Dissolve brown sugar in water and vinegar.

2. Add prunes, cinnamon, and pickling spice. Bring to a boil. Reduce heat; cover, simmer 10 minutes. Cool.

3. Add onion rings. Refrigerate at least 24 hours to fully plump prunes and develop flavor.

4. Serve on relish trays or as an accompaniment to ham, roast veal, pork, or poultry.

CURRIED FRUIT CASSEROLES

Yield: 50 portions

Ingredients

PRUNES, 40 to 50 COUNT	150 (3 pounds)
PEAR HALVES, drained	50 (1 No. 10 can)
CLING PEACH HALVES, drained	50 (1 No. 10 can)
PINEAPPLE SLICES, drained	50 (1 No. 10 can)
SUGAR, DARK BROWN	1 pound, 2 ounces
CURRY POWDER	3/4 cup
BUTTER, melted	1-1/2 pounds
ORANGE JUICE	1-1/2 quarts
ALMONDS, BLANCHED, SLIVERED	1-1/2 quarts

Procedure

1. Plump prunes in water, letting them stand overnight. Drain.

2. Arrange fruits in individual casseroles.

3. Mix brown sugar, curry powder, melted butter, and orange juice. Spoon 2 tablespoons of mixture over each casserole. Sprinkle each casserole with 1 tablespoon almonds.

4. Bake in oven at 350°F. for 15 to 20 minutes. Serve with chicken.

SPICED PURPLE PLUMS

Yield: 70 to 80

Ingredients

PURPLE PLUMS (IN HEAVY SYRUP)	1 No. 10 can
CINNAMON STICKS, 1-inch	4
PICKLING SPICE	2 tablespoons
CLOVES, WHOLE	1 tablespoon
MACE, GROUND	1 teaspoon
SUGAR	2 cups
VINEGAR	3/4 cup

Procedure

1. Drain plums, reserving 1 cup of syrup.
2. Tie cinnamon sticks, pickling spice, and cloves in a cheesecloth bag.
3. Combine mace, sugar, and vinegar. Add spice bag; bring to a boil.
4. Add reserved plum syrup. Boil 5 minutes. Remove spice bag.*
5. Pour hot spiced syrup over drained plums. Let stand until cold. Refrigerate overnight before using.

*For more pronounced spice flavor, do not remove spice bag until after plums and syrup are cold.

HOT SPICED FRUITS ———————➤

Yield: 25 portions (approximately 2 pineapple chunks and 1 other piece of fruit)

Ingredients

PINEAPPLE CHUNKS	1 1-pound, 4-ounce can
KUMQUATS, PRESERVED	1 1-pound, 4-ounce jar
VINEGAR	1/4 cup
SUGAR, BROWN, firmly packed	1/4 cup
CLOVES, WHOLE	1 teaspoon
CINNAMON STICKS, 3-inch	2
APRICOT HALVES	1 1-pound, 14-ounce can
PURPLE PLUMS	2 1-pound cans

PICKLED ORANGE SLICES

Yield: approximately 48 slices

Ingredients

ORANGES, LARGE, WHOLE	12
SALT	1 teaspoon
WATER	as needed
CLOVES, WHOLE	as needed
SUGAR	2 cups
CORN SYRUP, LIGHT	1/4 cup
VINEGAR	1 cup
WATER	1/2 cup
CINNAMON STICK, 2-inch	1

Procedure

1. Boil oranges with salt in water to cover for 1 hour. Drain and add fresh water twice during the hour of cooking. Drain.

2. Cut oranges into 1/2-inch slices; remove seeds if necessary. Insert 6 whole cloves in peel of each slice.

3. Combine sugar, corn syrup, vinegar, water, and cinnamon stick in a large shallow pan; boil 10 minutes.

4. Add orange slices to syrup; simmer 30 minutes, spooning syrup over oranges occasionally.

Procedure

1. Drain pineapple chunks and kumquats, reserving syrup. Combine syrup with vinegar, brown sugar, and spices. Bring to a boil; reduce heat; simmer 10 minutes.

2. Drain apricot halves and plums.

3. Add pineapple chunks, kumquats, apricot halves, and plums to the hot spiced syrup. Heat.

4. Serve as a garnish for ham, other meats, or poultry.

PINEAPPLE RELISH

Yield: approximately 1 gallon

Ingredients

PINEAPPLE, CRUSHED, PACKED IN JUICE	1 No. 10 can
HOT DOG RELISH	3 cups

Procedure

Combine ingredients. Serve 1 ounce per burger.

TIMELY RELISH

Yield: approximately 2 quarts

Ingredients

WHITE VINEGAR	1 cup
SUGAR	1 cup
SALT	1 teaspoon
MUSTARD SEED	1 tablespoon
CELERY SEED	1 teaspoon
AROMATIC BITTERS	2 teaspoons
APPLES	3
CELERY, diced	3 cups
GREEN PEPPER, finely chopped	2 cups
ONION, thinly sliced	1 cup

Procedure

1. Combine vinegar, sugar, and salt. Stir over low heat until sugar is dissolved; cool. Add mustard seed, celery seed, and bitters.

2. Peel, core, and dice apples into salted water to preserve color. Drain.

3. Combine apples, celery, green pepper, and onion. Add vinegar mixture; blend well. Store, covered, in refrigerator.

RAISIN RELISH GOURMET

Yield: approximately 2-3/4 quarts

Ingredients

RAISINS	2 cups
APPLES, TART, or CELERY, finely chopped	1-1/2 cups
GREEN ONIONS, finely chopped	1/2 cup
DILL, DRIED	1/2 teaspoon
SEASONED SALT	1 tablespoon
CHILI SAUCE	3/4 cup
SOUR CREAM	2 quarts

Procedure

1. Combine all ingredients.
2. Refrigerate several hours to blend flavors. Serve with broiled, baked, or panfried fish.

JIFFY RAISIN RELISH

Yield: 1 gallon

Ingredients

RAISINS, LIGHT or DARK	2 quarts
INSTANT MINCED ONION	1/4 cup
OR	
ONION, minced	1 cup
CHILI POWDER	4 teaspoons
CHILI SAUCE	1-1/2 quarts
WATER	1 quart

Procedure

1. Combine raisins, instant minced onion, and chili powder.
2. Combine chili sauce and water; bring to a boil; pour over raisin mixture. Let stand at least 1 hour, stirring occasionally.

PINEAPPLE VINAIGRETTE

Yield: 50 portions

Ingredients

GREEN BEANS, ITALIAN, FROZEN	3 pounds
PINEAPPLE CHUNKS	1 No. 10 can
PICKLES, SWEET, MIXED	2 quarts
PINEAPPLE SYRUP	2/3 cup
PICKLE SYRUP	2/3 cup
WINE VINEGAR	2-1/2 cups
SALAD OIL	1-1/4 cups
DILL WEED	1-1/4 teaspoons
LIQUID HOT PEPPER SEASONING	1/2 teaspoon
GARLIC SALT	1-1/4 teaspoons
GREEN PEPPER, cut in thin strips	1 quart
CELERY, thinly sliced	1-1/4 quarts
TOMATO WEDGES or CHERRY TOMATOES, halved	as needed

Procedure

1. Cook beans according to package directions until crisp-tender. Drain; cool.

2. Drain pineapple and pickles, reserving required amount of syrup.

3. Combine pineapple syrup, pickle syrup, vinegar, salad oil, dill, liquid hot pepper seasoning, and garlic salt; blend well.

4. Combine cooled beans, pineapple chunks, pickles, green pepper, and celery. Toss gently with dressing.

5. Cover; chill several hours.

6. Garnish with tomato. Serve as an accompaniment to cold meats.

SWEET AND SNAPPY RELISH

Yield: approximately 96 1-1/2-ounce portions

Ingredients

APPLESAUCE	1 No. 10 can
CURRANT JELLY	1/2 No. 10 can
PREPARED MUSTARD	3/4 cup

Procedure

Combine ingredients, mixing well; chill.

BARTLETT PEAR BAKE

Yield: 25 to 30 portions

Ingredients

BARTLETT PEAR HALVES, 25 to 30 COUNT	1 No. 10 can
PEAR SYRUP	1-1/2 cups
ORANGE JUICE from	1 orange
ORANGE PEEL grated, from	1 orange
CINNAMON STICKS	2
CURRY POWDER	1/2 teaspoon
NUTMEG, GROUND	1 teaspoon
SUGAR, BROWN	1/2 cup
CORNSTARCH	1 tablespoon

Procedure

1. Drain pear halves, reserving required amount of syrup. Place drained fruit in baking pan.

2. Combine pear syrup, orange juice, orange peel, spices, and brown sugar; blend with cornstarch.

3. Bring to a boil; cook and stir until clear. Pour over pears.

4. Bake in oven at 350°F. until heated through and fruit has taken on a glaze.

5. Serve with lamb, roast duck, or pork.

APPLESAUCE-PIMIENTO RELISH

Yield: 4-1/4 quarts; 96 1-1/2-ounce portions

Ingredients

APPLESAUCE	1 No. 10 can
SWEET PICKLES, finely diced	1-1/2 quarts
PIMIENTO, finely diced	2 cups
CELERY, diced	3 cups
ONION, finely chopped	1-1/2 cups

Procedure

Combine all ingredients. Mix well. Chill before serving.

MATCHLESS MARASCHINO RELISH

Yield: 50 to 60 portions

Ingredients

GELATINE, UNFLAVORED	3/4 ounce
MARASCHINO CHERRY JUICE	1-1/2 cups
LEMON JUICE	3 tablespoons
MANDARIN ORANGE JUICE	1 cup
WATER, boiling	3 cups
SWEET PICKLE RELISH	1 cup
MARASCHINO CHERRIES, chopped	3 cups
MANDARIN ORANGE SEGMENTS,	
CANNED, chopped	3 cups
CARDAMOM, GROUND	1 teaspoon
GINGER, GROUND	1 teaspoon

Procedure

1. Soften gelatine in cold maraschino cherry juice. Add lemon juice and mandarin orange juice.
2. Add boiling water, using rotary beater to mix thoroughly. Cool.
3. Add remaining ingredients. Mix well, refrigerate.
4. Serve as a relish with meat or poultry.

SPICY APPLESAUCE RELISH

Yield: 100 1-1/2-ounce portions

Ingredients

APPLESAUCE	1 No. 10 can
RED CINNAMON CANDIES (IMPERIALS)	2 cups (1 pound)
CELERY, diced	3 cups
RAISINS, SEEDLESS	3 cups (1 pound)
PREPARED HORSERADISH	3/4 cup

Procedure

1. Heat about half of the applesauce. Add cinnamon candies; stir to dissolve. Cool.
2. Combine with remaining applesauce, celery, raisins, and horseradish; chill several hours before serving.

CURRIED PEARS

Yield: 40 to 50 portions

Ingredients

PEAR HALVES	1 No. 10 can
PEAR SYRUP	1 quart
SUGAR	1/2 cup
CORNSTARCH	3 tablespoons
WATER, cold	1 cup
GINGER, GROUND	1 teaspoon
CURRY POWDER	2 teaspoons

Procedure

1. Drain pears, reserving syrup. Arrange pears in counter pan.

2. Combine required amount of syrup and sugar; bring to a boil.

3. Blend cornstarch in water; add to hot liquid. Cook, stirring, until clear.

4. Stir in spices; remove from heat.

5. Pour syrup over pears in pan; let stand 30 minutes to 1 hour before serving.

CALYPSO RELISH

Yield: approximately 1 quart

Ingredients

PINEAPPLE, CRUSHED	1 No. 2 can
PINEAPPLE JUICE and VINEGAR to equal	1 cup
CINNAMON STICK, 3-inch	1
SALT	1 teaspoon
WHOLE-CRANBERRY SAUCE	1 1-pound can
CELERY, finely chopped	1 cup
ONION, finely chopped	1/4 cup
AROMATIC BITTERS	2 teaspoons

Procedure

1. Drain pineapple. Measure juice; add vinegar to make required amount. Add cinnamon stick, broken into pieces. Cook over medium heat until liquid is reduced by half. Add salt; cool; strain.

2. Combine strained liquid, pineapple, cranberry sauce, celery, onion, and bitters; blend well. Chill.

CURRY PINEAPPLE RELISH

Yield: 2-1/2 quarts

Ingredients

PINEAPPLE, CRUSHED (IN EXTRA HEAVY SYRUP)	1 No. 10 can
SUGAR, BROWN	12 ounces
BUTTER or MARGARINE	1/2 pound
VINEGAR	1 cup
CURRY POWDER	3 tablespoons
SALT	2 tablespoons
GARLIC POWDER	1 teaspoon

Procedure

1. Drain pineapple.

2. Combine drained fruit, brown sugar, butter, vinegar, curry powder, salt, and garlic powder. Simmer 10 minutes.

3. Serve warm with fried breaded fish, lamb, pork, chicken, or ham.

Jam and Jelly Bases for Garnishes

Advisory Council for Jams, Jellies and Preserves

Vegetable Relishes

RELISH PLATTERS

Yield: 48 portions

Ingredients

RADISHES	48
CARROTS	1 pound
CELERY HEARTS	48
CHERRY TOMATOES	48
MELONS (HONEYDEWS preferable)	4
LETTUCE LEAVES	8
MINT, 3-inch pieces	24 pieces

Procedure

1. Make radish roses, carrot strips, and celery hearts at least 2 hours in advance of serving. Refrigerate in cold water and cracked ice.

2. Wash cherry tomatoes; chill.

3. Cut melons in half; remove seeds. Reserve one half of each melon to use in center of platter as "cup" for carrot strips. Peel the other 4 halves and cut in finger-length pieces.

4. Place 2 lettuce leaves on each of 4, 13-inch platters; place melon half in center and fill with carrot strips. Garnish with mint. Arrange the radish roses, remainder of carrot strips, celery hearts, cherry tomatoes, and melon strips around melon half. Garnish with remainder of mint.

SAVORY MUSHROOMS

Yield: 3-1/2 cups

Ingredients

PICKLES, SLICED	
BREAD AND BUTTER	1 15-ounce jar
MUSHROOMS, SLICED, drained	1 8-ounce can

Procedure

1. Drain pickles, reserving liquid.

2. Pour spiced liquid from pickles over mushrooms. Heat to boiling; cool.

3. Add pickles; mix; chill.

CORN RELISH

Yield: approximately 3 quarts

Ingredients

ONION, chopped	2 cups
CELERY SEED	2-1/2 tablespoons
MUSTARD SEED	1 tablespoon
VINEGAR	2 cups
SALT	2 tablespoons
SUGAR	2 cups
CORN, CANNED, WHOLE KERNEL, drained	2 quarts
SWEET PICKLE RELISH	1 cup
PIMIENTO, diced	1-1/2 cups
CELERY, chopped	2 cups

Procedure

1. Combine onion, celery seed, mustard seed, vinegar, salt, and sugar; bring to a boil. Reduce heat; simmer 10 minutes.
2. Combine corn, pickle relish, pimiento, and celery.
3. Add hot liquid to the corn mixture, mixing well. Cool.
4. Chill at least 24 hours for flavors to blend.

GOLDEN CORN RELISH

Yield: 48 1/4-cup portions

Ingredients

CORN, CANNED, WHOLE KERNEL, drained	1-3/4 quarts
GREEN PEPPER, chopped	1-1/3 cups
PIMIENTO, chopped	1/2 cup
CELERY, chopped	2 cups
ONION, finely chopped	2 cups
BLACK PEPPER	1/4 teaspoon
ITALIAN SALAD DRESSING, BOTTLED	1 quart

Procedure

Combine all ingredients. Chill several hours before serving.

Note

This is a fresh relish. Keep under refrigeration.

KRAUT CORN RELISH

Yield: 1-1/2 quarts

Ingredients

OLIVE or SALAD OIL	2 tablespoons
ONION, LARGE, sliced	1
GREEN PEPPER, diced	1 cup
SAUERKRAUT	3 cups
CORN, WHOLE KERNEL	1-1/2 cups
TOMATOES, cut in wedges	2
SUGAR, BROWN	1/4 cup
WINE VINEGAR	2 tablespoons
PARSLEY FLAKES	1 tablespoon
CELERY SEED	2 teaspoons
SEASONED SALT	1 teaspoon
DRY MUSTARD	1/2 teaspoon
BLACK PEPPER	1/4 teaspoon

Procedure

1. Heat oil. Add onion and green pepper; cook over low heat until tender.

2. Add remaining ingredients; stir.

3. Cover; cook over low heat, stirring occasionally, for 25 minutes. Cool.

CORN SALAD

Yield: 24 4-ounce portions

Ingredients

CORN, WHOLE KERNEL (VACUUM PACK)	1 75-ounce can
PIMIENTO, chopped	1 cup
GREEN PEPPER, chopped	2 cups
GREEN ONIONS, finely sliced	2 cups
CUCUMBERS, diced	2 cups
COLORLESS FRENCH DRESSING*	1 quart

Procedure

Combine vegetables. Add French Dressing; toss to mix.

*See recipe, page 66.

MARINATED CARROT WHEELS

Yield: 10 pounds

Ingredients

CARROTS, peeled	10 pounds
SALT	2 tablespoons
COLORLESS FRENCH DRESSING*	1 quart plus 1 cup
PARSLEY, minced	as needed

Procedure

1. Score carrots lengthwise with dinner fork. Slice crosswise in 1/4-inch slices. Spread in perforated steamer pan; steam 5 minutes only. They should be crisp-tender. Cool.

2. Place cooled carrots in flat pan. Sprinkle with salt. Pour dressing over; allow to stand 2 to 3 hours, stirring gently several times.

3. Use carrot wheels alone in bowl with minced parsley on top. Or, mix with marinated cauliflower; add minced parsley garnish.

*COLORLESS FRENCH DRESSING

Yield: 1 gallon

Ingredients

SALT	4 ounces
DRY MUSTARD	2 ounces
SUGAR, CONFECTIONERS'	2 ounces
CAYENNE PEPPER	few grains
LEMON JUICE	1-1/2 cups
SALAD OIL	2-3/4 quarts
VINEGAR	3 cups

Procedure

1. Sift salt, mustard, sugar, and cayenne pepper into mixer bowl.

2. Add enough lemon juice to make a paste; beat until smooth.

3. Add oil gradually, beating on high speed.

4. Turn to second speed. Add remaining lemon juice and the vinegar; beat thoroughly.

5. Store in covered container. Mix well before using.

VEGETABLE COTTAGE CHEESE

Yield: 25 1/2-cup portions

Ingredients

CUCUMBERS, finely chopped	3 cups (1 pound)
RADISHES, finely chopped	3/4 cup
GREEN ONIONS, finely chopped	1/3 cup
CELERY, finely chopped	1-1/2 cups
GREEN PEPPER, finely chopped	1 cup
COTTAGE CHEESE	5 cups (2-1/2 pounds)
SALT	1-1/2 teaspoons
MAYONNAISE	1/4 cup

Procedure

1. Prepare vegetables, leaving a portion of the green stems on the onions.

2. Combine vegetables, cottage cheese, salt, and mayonnaise. Blend well. Chill.

SWEETENED KRAUT RELISH

Yield: 50 portions

Ingredients

SAUERKRAUT, undrained	1 No. 10 can
SUGAR, BROWN	1 pound, 2 ounces
CELERY SEED	1 tablespoon
CARAWAY SEED	1 tablespoon
SALT	1 tablespoon

Procedure

1. Drain kraut thoroughly, reserving all liquid.

2. Combine kraut liquid with remaining ingredients. Heat to boiling; simmer 2 to 3 minutes.

3. Pour hot liquid over kraut; mix well. Chill thoroughly.

KRAUT SLAW ELEGANTE ⟶

Yield: 50 portions

Ingredients

SAUERKRAUT, drained	1 No. 10 can
CHEESE, AMERICAN, shredded	1-1/2 pounds
ONION, sliced	1 pound
MAYONNAISE or SALAD DRESSING	1 quart
PINEAPPLE CHUNKS, drained	1 quart
PIMIENTO, chopped	1-1/2 cups

EGGPLANT RELISH

Yield: approximately 2 quarts

Ingredients

EGGPLANT, MEDIUM-SIZED	1
OLIVE OIL	1/2 cup
GREEN PEPPER, MEDIUM-SIZED, coarsely chopped	1
ONION, coarsely chopped	1/2 cup
GARLIC, crushed	2 cloves
RED WINE VINEGAR	1/4 cup
TOMATO PASTE	2 cups
MUSHROOMS, STEMS AND PIECES	1 4-ounce can
WATER	1 cup
OLIVES, SMALL, GREEN, PIMIENTO-STUFFED	1 cup
SUGAR	1 tablespoon
OREGANO	1/2 teaspoon
SEASONED SALT	1 teaspoon
BLACK PEPPER, coarsely ground	1/4 teaspoon

Procedure

1. Cut peeled eggplant into 1-inch cubes. Combine with olive oil, green pepper, onion, and garlic. Cover; cook gently until eggplant is tender, stirring occasionally.

2. Add vinegar, tomato paste, mushrooms with liquid, water, olives, sugar, and seasonings; mix well. Simmer 15 to 20 minutes.

3. Cover; chill overnight to blend flavors.

Procedure

1. Cut drained kraut in short lengths.

2. Combine with remaining ingredients; chill thoroughly.

3. Serve with hot or cold sliced ham or chicken or with broiled or baked fish.

EGGPLANT AND PICKLED VEGETABLES

Yield: approximately 3-3/4 quarts

Ingredients

EGGPLANT, LARGE	2
OLIVE OIL	3/4 cup
GARLIC, crushed	1 clove
ONION, chopped	1 cup
ITALIAN PLUM TOMATOES	1 can (1 pound, 13 ounces)
TOMATO SAUCE	1 cup
GREEN PEPPER, sliced	2 cups
CELERY, sliced	2 cups
PARSLEY, chopped	1/4 cup
BASIL	1 teaspoon
BLACK PEPPER	1/4 teaspoon
SALT	2 teaspoons
SUGAR	2 tablespoons
WINE VINEGAR	1/4 cup
CAPERS	1/4 cup
OLIVES, GREEN, PIMIENTO-STUFFED, sliced	2/3 cup

Procedure

1. Cut unpeeled eggplant into 1-inch cubes. Brown in olive oil. Remove from pan; drain on paper towels.

2. Saute garlic and onion in pan, adding a little more oil if necessary.

3. Add tomatoes, tomato sauce, green pepper, celery, parsley, basil, pepper, and salt. Cover; simmer 15 minutes.

4. Add eggplant, sugar, vinegar, capers, and olives. Cover; simmer 15 minutes.

5. Refrigerate, covered, overnight to blend flavors.

CABBAGE RELISH NO. 1

Yield: 25 portions

Ingredients

CABBAGE, finely chopped	3 quarts (2 pounds)
GREEN PEPPER, diced	3/4 cup
RED PEPPERS, diced	1/3 cup
ONION, finely chopped (optional)	2 tablespoons
SUGAR	1/2 cup
SALT	1 tablespoon
BLACK PEPPER	3/4 teaspoon
DRY MUSTARD	2 teaspoons
CELERY SEED	1 tablespoon
VINEGAR	1-1/2 cups
SALAD OIL	3/4 cup

Procedure

1. Combine vegetables.

2. Mix seasonings and vinegar; stir until sugar is dissolved. Add salad oil.

3. Pour dressing over vegetable mixture; toss together until thoroughly mixed. Cover and chill.

BEET RELISH

Yield: 2-1/2 quarts

Ingredients

BEETS, DICED or JULIENNE	1 No. 10 can
INSTANT MINCED ONION	1/3 cup
OR	
ONION, finely chopped	1-1/3 cups
LEMON JUICE	1-1/4 cups
SUGAR	1/3 cup
SALT	1 tablespoon
CELERY SEED	2 teaspoons

Procedure

1. Drain beets. Mix all remaining ingredients; pour over beets; mix lightly.

2. Let stand 24 hours in refrigerator before serving.

CABBAGE RELISH NO. 2

Yield: approximately 1 gallon

Ingredients

OLIVES, RIPE	3 cups
CABBAGE, finely shredded	2 quarts
CELERY, thinly sliced	1 quart
GREEN PEPPER, shredded	1-1/2 cups
SWEET RED PEPPERS, shredded	1-1/2 cups
INSTANT MINCED ONION	1/4 cup
VINEGAR	1-1/2 cups
WATER	2-1/4 cups
SUGAR	2/3 cup
CELERY SEED	1 tablespoon
SALT	2 teaspoons
BLACK PEPPER	1/4 teaspoon

Procedure

1. Cut olives into wedges. Combine with vegetables.

2. Combine onion, vinegar, water, sugar, celery seed, salt, and pepper. Add to vegetable mixture. Let stand for several hours.

RELISH TRAY CARROTS

Yield: approximately 20 portions

Ingredients

CARROTS, thinly sliced or cut julienne	2 pounds
GARLIC, minced	3 or 4 cloves
SALT	1 teaspoon
BLACK PEPPER	1/4 teaspoon
OLIVE OIL	4 tablespoons
TARRAGON VINEGAR	1/2 cup
OREGANO	1/2 teaspoon

Procedure

1. Boil carrots in water until barely tender. Do not overcook. Drain well.

2. Make a dressing of remaining ingredients; pour over hot, well-drained carrots.

3. Refrigerate 6 to 12 hours before serving.

MIXED VEGETABLE RELISH

Yield: 36 portions

Ingredients

WAX BEANS, CUT	2 No. 2 cans
GREEN BEANS, CUT	2 No. 2 cans
RED KIDNEY BEANS	2 No. 2 cans
GREEN PEPPER, chopped	1/2 cup
CELERY, chopped	2 cups
ONION, grated	2 tablespoons
SALAD OIL	1-1/2 cups
VINEGAR	2/3 cup
SUGAR	1/2 cup
SALT	2 teaspoons
BLACK PEPPER	1/4 teaspoon

Procedure

   1. Drain canned vegetables.

   2. Combine drained vegetables, green pepper, celery, and onion.

   3. Mix oil, vinegar, and seasonings. Pour over vegetables; toss lightly; chill.

DUTCH BEAN RELISH

Yield: approximately 1 gallon

Ingredients

SAUERKRAUT, drained	2 quarts (3 pounds)
GREEN BEANS, DIAGONAL CUT, drained	1 No. 10 can
PIMIENTO, diced	1 cup
SUGAR	1/2 cup
SALT	2-1/2 teaspoons
MUSTARD SEED	2-1/2 teaspoons
VINEGAR	2-1/2 cups
WATER	2-1/2 cups

Procedure

   1. Chop sauerkraut to shorten shreds. Combine with green beans and pimiento; toss gently but thoroughly. Spread evenly in a flat pan.

   2. Combine sugar, salt, mustard seed, vinegar, and water; bring to a boil. Reduce heat; simmer about 5 minutes.

   3. Pour hot liquid over vegetable mixture; cool slightly. Refrigerate several hours or overnight, mixing occasionally.

RIPE OLIVE RELISH

Yield: 2 quarts

Ingredients

OLIVES, RIPE, PITTED	2 cups
PIMIENTO, finely chopped	4 ounces
GREEN ONIONS, chopped	3/4 cup (3 ounces)
CELERY, chopped	1 cup (4 ounces)
PEANUTS, chopped	3 ounces
CABBAGE, finely shredded	1 pound, 2 ounces
SALAD OIL	1/4 cup
VINEGAR	2 tablespoons
SALT	2 teaspoons

Procedure

1. Chop olives coarsely. Mix with pimiento, green onions, celery, peanuts, and cabbage.

2. Add oil, vinegar, and salt. Toss to mix well.

3. Use as a relish in corned beef or pastrami sandwiches made with french rolls or use on hamburgers or as an accompaniment to cold meats.

CELERY AND APPLES INDIENNE

Yield: 48 portions

Ingredients

CELERY, sliced diagonally into 1-inch pieces	1-1/2 gallons
CHICKEN STOCK or WATER	1 quart
SALT	2 teaspoons
BUTTER or MARGARINE	1 pound
APPLES, unpeeled, sliced 1/4 inch thick	3 quarts
ONION, sliced	3 cups
CURRY POWDER	1/4 cup
SALT	2 teaspoons
SUGAR	3 tablespoons

Procedure

1. Combine celery, stock, and first amount of salt. Bring to a boil. Cover; cook until celery is crisp-tender, about 3 to 4 minutes.

2. Melt butter in a large skillet. Add apples, onion, curry powder, and remaining salt. Saute until apples are tender.

3. Add celery and sugar. Cook 1 to 2 minutes longer. Serve hot with meat or poultry.

OLIVE-BEAN RELISH

Yield: 4-1/2 quarts

Ingredients

OLIVES, RIPE, WHOLE, PITTED	2-1/2 cups
RED KIDNEY BEANS, CANNED or cooked	1-1/2 quarts
GREEN LIMA BEANS, CANNED or cooked	1-1/2 quarts
GARBANZO or CECI BEANS, CANNED or cooked	3 cups
ONION, LARGE (4 ounces)	1
GARLIC, minced	2 teaspoons
WHITE WINE VINEGAR	2 cups
SALAD OIL	2/3 cup
SUGAR	1/2 cup
SALT	2 teaspoons
PICKLING SPICE*	2 tablespoons

*Or use 1 teaspoon *each* of celery seed and mustard seed, 1 tablespoon whole allspice, 1 teaspoon peppercorns, and 1 bay leaf.

Procedure

1. Quarter olives. Rinse and drain kidney beans; drain limas and garbanzos. Mix olives and beans lightly in 12-inch by 20-inch by 2-1/2-inch pan.

2. Cut onion into rings. Combine in saucepan with garlic, vinegar, oil, sugar, salt, and spice. Bring to a boil; cover; simmer 5 minutes. Remove from heat; pour over vegetable mixture. Marinate at least 2 hours, stirring occasionally.

3. Serve as an antipasto, or as a vegetable relish with beef or veal.

Garden Fresh Relish Tray

United Fresh Fruit and Vegetable Association

SMOKY HOT DOG RELISH

Yield: 1-3/4 quarts

Ingredients

OLIVES, RIPE, CHOPPED	3 cups
CATSUP	1 quart
PREPARED MUSTARD	1 quart
INSTANT MINCED ONION	1/2 cup
SMOKE SALT	2 teaspoons
LIQUID HOT PEPPER SEASONING	1/4 teaspoon

Procedure

Mix all ingredients well. Chill.

FARMERS' CHOP SUEY

Yield: 16 portions

Ingredients

RADISHES	1 pound, 2 ounces
CUCUMBERS, peeled	1 pound, 3 ounces
CELERY	1 pound, 4 ounces
GREEN ONIONS	8 ounces
TOMATOES, FRESH, peeled	9 ounces
SOUR CREAM	6 ounces
SALT	2 teaspoons
WHITE PEPPER	1/2 teaspoon

Procedure

1. Cut radishes into quarters.
2. Cut cucumbers lengthwise in quarters, then cut across to make 1-inch pieces.
3. Cut celery into 1-inch pieces.
4. Slice onions finely.
5. Cut tomatoes into wedges.
6. Combine vegetables.
7. Mix sour cream with seasonings.
8. Just before serving, add dressing to vegetables; mix lightly but thoroughly.

Mint Gelatin Cubes Accent Lamb

American Lamb Council

Molded Relishes

SHERRY JELLY

Yield: 56 1-ounce portions

Ingredients

GELATINE, UNFLAVORED	1 ounce
SHERRY	6 cups
SUGAR	1-1/2 cups
SOUFFLE CUPS, No. 47	56

Procedure

1. Soften gelatine in 2 cups of the sherry. Dissolve over hot water.
2. Add remaining sherry and sugar; stir until sugar is dissolved.
3. Pour into souffle cups, allowing 2 tablespoons per cup. Chill until firm.

Note

Use sherry with a good body. If a lighter flavor is desired, use 2 cups of apple juice to soften gelatine and only 4 cups of sherry.

SPICED GRAPE RELISH

Yield: 20 3-ounce portions

Ingredients

GRAPE JUICE	1-1/2 quarts
CINNAMON STICK	1
CLOVES, WHOLE	1 tablespoon
WATER, hot	as needed
GELATIN, STRAWBERRY FLAVOR	1-3/4 cups
SALT	1/2 teaspoon

Procedure

1. Bring grape juice, cinnamon stick, and cloves to a boil. Strain; add hot water to make 2 quarts.
2. Dissolve gelatin and salt in hot liquid.
3. Turn into molds, allowing about 1/3 cup for each mold. Chill until firm.
4. Unmold. Serve in crisp lettuce cups, garnished with creamy mayonnaise.

JELLIED HORSERADISH CREAM

Yield: 1 12-inch by 20-inch by 2-inch pan; 60 portions

Ingredients

GELATINE, UNFLAVORED	1/2 cup
WATER, cold	1 quart
WATER, boiling	1 quart
CREAM, WHIPPING	2 quarts
SUGAR, CONFECTIONERS'	1/3 cup
SALT	2 teaspoons
HORSERADISH	1-1/2 cups

Procedure

1. Soften gelatine in cold water. Dissolve in boiling water. Chill until slightly thickened.

2. Whip cream; add sugar and salt slowly.

3. Blend horseradish into whipped cream. Fold mixture into gelatine. Refrigerate until firm.

4. Cut into squares. Serve in small lettuce cup with a garnish of chopped parsley or strips of pimiento. Use with ham, corned beef, or roast beef sandwiches.

REGAL HORSERADISH CREAM RELISH

Yield: 1-1/4 gallons

Ingredients

GELATIN, LEMON FLAVOR	1-1/2 pounds
SALT	2 tablespoons
WATER, hot	2 quarts
WHITE PEPPER	1 teaspoon
ONION, grated	2 tablespoons
PREPARED HORSERADISH	2 cups
SOUR CREAM	2 quarts

Procedure

1. Dissolve gelatin and salt in hot water.

2. Add remaining ingredients; stir until well blended. Pour into individual molds, or into shallow pans to a depth of 1-1/2 inches.

3. Chill until firm.

4. Unmold or cut into squares. Serve on crisp salad greens.

MOLDED PIQUANT FRUIT RELISH

Yield: 1-1/2 gallons; 64 3-ounce portions

Ingredients

GELATINE, UNFLAVORED	2 ounces
WATER, cold	1-1/2 cups
APPLESAUCE	1 No. 10 can
SUGAR	1-1/2 cups
CIDER VINEGAR	1-1/2 cups
PREPARED HORSERADISH	1/3 cup
SALT	1 tablespoon
RAISINS	1-1/2 cups
CELERY, diced	3 cups
CABBAGE, finely shredded	3 cups

Procedure

1. Soften gelatine in cold water.

2. Heat applesauce. Add softened gelatine; stir until dissolved. Add sugar, vinegar, horseradish, and salt. Cool.

3. Add raisins, celery, and cabbage; mix well. Pour into small individual molds or into shallow pans. Chill until set.

4. Unmold or cut into squares. Serve on lettuce or other salad greens. If desired, garnish with mayonnaise flavored slightly with prepared horseradish.

CIDER AND CRANBERRY RELISH

Yield: 46 3-ounce portions

Ingredients

GELATIN, STRAWBERRY FLAVOR	1-1/2 pounds
SUGAR	1 cup
SALT	2 teaspoons
SWEET CIDER, hot	1-3/4 quarts
CRANBERRY JUICE COCKTAIL	2 quarts

Procedure

1. Dissolve gelatin, sugar, and salt in hot cider.

2. Add cranberry juice cocktail. Turn into small individual molds, or into pans to a depth of 1-1/4 inches. Chill until firm.

3. Unmold or cut in squares.

JELLIED PIMIENTO RELISH

Yield: 42 3-ounce portions

Ingredients

GELATIN, LEMON FLAVOR	2-1/3 cups (1 pound)
SALT	1 teaspoon
SWEET PICKLE JUICE and	
WATER, hot to equal	2-1/2 quarts
VINEGAR	1/2 cup
PIMIENTO, chopped	2 cups
SWEET PICKLES, chopped	1-1/4 quarts

Procedure

    1. Dissolve gelatin and salt in hot liquid. Add vinegar.

    2. Chill until slightly thickened. Fold in pimiento and pickles.

    3. Turn into individual molds, or into shallow pans to a depth of 1-1/4 inches. Chill until firm. Unmold or cut in 2-inch squares. Serve on lettuce with mayonnaise.

CUCUMBER RELISH MOLD

Yield: 24 portions

Ingredients

GELATINE, UNFLAVORED	1/4 cup (1 ounce)
WATER, cold	3 cups
ONION, minced	1/4 cup
SALT	1-1/2 tablespoons
SUGAR	1-1/2 tablespoons
CUCUMBERS, peeled, grated	1 quart
SOUR CREAM	1 quart
HORSERADISH	4 to 6 tablespoons
VINEGAR	1/2 cup
LIQUID HOT PEPPER SEASONING	dash

Procedure

    1. Soften gelatine in cold water. Add onion, salt, and sugar.

    2. Stir over low heat until gelatine dissolves. Cool.

    3. Add cucumbers, sour cream, horseradish, vinegar, and liquid hot pepper seasoning.

    4. Pour into individual molds. Chill until firm.

    5. Unmold. Serve on crisp salad greens. Garnish with radish roses, if desired.

JELLIED APRICOTS IN SHERRY

Yield: 42 3-ounce portions

Ingredients

GELATIN, RASPBERRY FLAVOR	2-1/3 cups (1 pound)
SALT	1/2 teaspoon
WATER, hot	1-3/4 quarts
SHERRY	2 cups
APRICOT HALVES, CANNED, drained	42
APPLES, finely diced	1-1/2 quarts

Procedure

1. Dissolve gelatin and salt in hot water. Cool. Add sherry. Chill until slightly thickened.

2. Place apricots, cut-side up, in small individual molds.

3. Add apples to slightly thickened gelatin; turn into molds over apricots. Chill until firm.

4. Unmold on lettuce.

JELLIED CRANBERRY CHUTNEY

Yield: 64 2-ounce portions

Ingredients

WHOLE CRANBERRY SAUCE	1-1/2 quarts (3-1/2 pounds)
SUGAR, BROWN, firmly packed	1/2 cup (3 ounces)
VINEGAR	1/4 cup
RAISINS	1 cup
ALMONDS, CHOPPED	1 cup (4 ounces)
GARLIC SALT	1 teaspoon
GINGER	1 teaspoon
CAYENNE PEPPER	1/4 to 1/2 teaspoon
GELATIN, LEMON FLAVOR	1-3/4 cups (12 ounces)
WATER, hot	1-1/2 quarts

Procedure

1. Combine cranberry sauce, brown sugar, vinegar, raisins, almonds, and seasonings; let stand to combine flavors.

2. Dissolve gelatin in hot water. Chill until slightly thickened. Fold in cranberry mixture.

3. Pour into 2-ounce molds; chill until firm.

MOLDED SPICED PEACH RELISH

Yield: 42 3-ounce portions

Ingredients

PEACHES, CANNED, SLICED, undrained	1-3/4 quarts
VINEGAR	1-1/2 cups
SUGAR	3 cups
CINNAMON STICKS	1-1/2 ounces
CLOVES, WHOLE	1-1/2 tablespoons
WATER, hot	as needed
GELATIN, ORANGE FLAVOR	2-1/3 cups (1 pound)

Procedure

1. Drain peaches, reserving juice. Combine juice, vinegar, sugar, and spices (tied in cheesecloth bag). Bring to a boil.

2. Add peaches; cover; simmer 10 minutes.

3. Remove spices. Drain peaches, reserving syrup. Measure syrup; add hot water to make 2-3/4 quarts.

4. Dissolve gelatin in the hot liquid. Chill until slightly thickened. Fold in peaches.

5. Turn into rectangular pans to a depth of 1-1/4 inches, or into small individual molds. Chill until firm. Cut in small cubes or unmold. Serve a few cubes or an individual mold nested in lettuce or chicory.

MOLDED MUSTARD RELISH

Yield: 60 1-ounce portions

Ingredients

GELATINE, UNFLAVORED	3/4 ounce
WATER, cold	1-1/2 cups
SUGAR	1/2 cup
SALT	1-1/2 teaspoons
DRY MUSTARD	3 tablespoons
TURMERIC	1 teaspoon
MILK	1 cup
MAYONNAISE	2 cups
VINEGAR	1/2 cup
CREAM, WHIPPING	1-1/2 cups
SOUFFLE CUPS, No. 47	60
PARSLEY, chopped	as needed

Procedure

1. Soften gelatine in cold water. Dissolve over hot water.

2. Combine sugar, salt, mustard, and turmeric; add to gelatine; stir until dissolved.

3. Add milk, mayonnaise, and vinegar; blend well. Chill until mixture mounds slightly when dropped from a spoon.

4. Whip cream. Fold carefully into gelatine mixture.

5. Spoon mixture into souffle cups. Chill until firm. Garnish with chopped parsley, if desired.

Seafood Salads with Garnishes and Sauces

National Fisheries Institute

SAUCES

SAUCES ARE an essential part of good cookery. Chosen with understanding, they lend interest and distinction. They complement, enhance, and impart a certain elegance to the very best of food.

As the art of making sauces has developed, more and more kinds of sauces have been created. The French, particularly, mastered this branch of cookery to a notable degree. It is, in large measure, due to their efforts that the world of today has its heritage of fine sauces.

There are, of course, exceptions. There are some great German sauces, for instance, and others from Italy and Spain. The assorted tomato sauces, dissimilar as they are, have had their beginnings in separate regions—in Italy, in France, or in Mexico. Fruit sauces are usually Teutonic or Scandinavian in origin.

The various kinds of sauces, when arranged in a logical pattern, are not unlike a family tree. There are a few foundation or "mother" sauces from which derive a whole series of re-

lated types that are created by the addition of wine, herbs, seasonings, or piquant ingredients of sundry kinds.

White sauce and brown sauce are two examples of this "mother" group. Both sauces are thickened by roux (equal parts of fat and flour, heated together). For white sauce, the pale, delicately flavored stock from veal, chicken, or fish is used. However, milk, or a combination of milk and stock, serves as the liquid in some recipes. In the preparation of these sauces the color of the roux remains white throughout the heating step. The brown sauces have a robust brown stock as their base, and the roux is browned to the degree that the flour is allowed to "roast" during heating.

Other foundation sauces include the butter sauces (which are essentially seasoned butter) and the mayonnaises which are made with egg yolk and oil or butter. (With oil, these sauces are known as mayonnaise; with butter, hollandaise.)

Beyond these there is a large group of assorted sauces that may be classified in different ways. Some authorities lump them together and call them cold and hot "special sauces." Others separate them into 2 groups: (1) barbecue sauces, comprised of various sauces that are heavily seasoned, usually with vinegar; and, (2) miscellaneous sauces, including the tomato and fruit sauces. For this book, we have elected to expand the number of categories and classify the list in a more complete detail.

In the French domain, sauce-making has always been regarded as a worthy art and treated as a serious matter. According to tradition, expert preparation requires knowledge, practiced skill, and a long, painstaking procedure. In our country, conditions are somewhat different; different thoughts prevail. With today's pressure for time, shortcuts are expedient, often necessary. Many products have been devised to shorten the labor time needed for sauce-making. Meat extracts, clear and cream soups, soup bases, tomato products, seasoning combinations, and other prepared items are available to simplify and speed preparation.

But regardless of the method used or the time taken to prepare a sauce, certain basic rules apply:

1. Choose sauces carefully from the standpoint of compatibility with the character of the food they are intended to

*enhance, giving special consideration to flavors and textures.
(There should be an intimate and harmonious relation between food and sauce.)*

*2. Prepare (and, if necessary, adjust) thickened sauces to
maintain a "just right" consistency—neither too runny nor
too thick. As a guideline, a sauce of this type should be thick
enough to have sufficient "body" to lightly coat the food.*

*3. Establish a proper relationship between proportions of
sauce and food. Ideally, portions of sauce and food should
agree so that, without any hint of over-saucing, there is a sufficient amount of sauce to accompany the last bite of food.*

Frionor Norwegian

*A spicy tomato and green pepper sauce for fried fish is
accented with a garnish of peaches studded with cloves.*

Cocktail Sauces

COCKTAIL SAUCE

Yield: 50 portions

Ingredients

CHILI SAUCE	1-1/2 quarts
LEMON JUICE	1/2 cup
PREPARED HORSERADISH	1/4 cup
LIQUID HOT PEPPER SEASONING	1/2 teaspoon or to taste

Procedure

Combine all ingredients. Chill.

SPICY RED SAUCE

Yield: 2-1/8 quarts

Ingredients

CATSUP	2 quarts
DRY MUSTARD	3 tablespoons
LIQUID HOT PEPPER SEASONING	1 teaspoon
WORCESTERSHIRE SAUCE	1/4 cup
MACE, GROUND	1 teaspoon

Procedure

1. Combine all ingredients.
2. Serve at room temperature.

REMOULADE SAUCE

Yield: approximately 1 quart

Ingredients

MAYONNAISE	3-1/2 cups
GARLIC, crushed	2 cloves
DRY MUSTARD	1 tablespoon
TARRAGON, DRY	3/4 teaspoon
PARSLEY, minced	1/4 cup
PICKLES, SOUR, finely chopped	1/2 cup
CAPERS, chopped	1-1/2 tablespoons

Procedure

Combine all ingredients, mixing thoroughly. Let stand in refrigerator for at least 1/2 hour to blend flavors. Serve cold.

Gravies

AU JUS–NATURAL JUICE

Yield: 2 quarts

Ingredients
No. 1 (using pan drippings in roast pan)

WATER	2 quarts
CATSUP	1/4 cup
WORCESTERSHIRE SAUCE	2 tablespoons
BUTTER	3 ounces
SALT	as needed
CARAMEL COLORING	as needed
CORNSTARCH	2 ounces

No. 2 (only when pan drippings are not available)

WATER	2 quarts
CATSUP	1/4 cup
WORCESTERSHIRE SAUCE	2 tablespoons
BUTTER	3 ounces
BEEF BASE	3 ounces
SALT	1/2 ounce
CARAMEL COLORING	as needed
CORNSTARCH	2 ounces

Procedure

1. Add water, catsup, Worcestershire sauce, and butter to roast pan. (For No. 2, put these ingredients into pot; add beef base.)

2. Bring to boil; add salt and caramel coloring to make a light coffee color.

3. Moisten cornstarch with cold water. Add to pan; stir until smooth; simmer 5 minutes. Strain into steam table pot. Keep hot (160°F.) at all times on steam table.

Note

Use accurate weight on cornstarch. Au Jus should be consistency of half-and-half coffee cream.

CHICKEN GRAVY

Yield: 2 gallons

Ingredients

CHICKEN STOCK	2 gallons
CHICKEN FAT (skimmed from stock)	2 pounds
FLOUR, HARD WHEAT	1-1/4 pounds
SALT	as needed
YELLOW FOOD COLORING	2 to 4 drops

Procedure

1. Heat stock; strain through fine strainer.

2. Skim fat from top of stock; put fat in saucepan. Boil until stock has evaporated from fat. Do not brown. Add shortening to fat, if necessary, to make up required amount.

3. Add flour; blend. Whip until very smooth; simmer 10 minutes over low heat. Do not brown flour.

4. Bring stock to a boil. Add roux to stock; whip until very smooth. Simmer 10 minutes.

5. Check seasoning. Add salt, if necessary, and yellow food coloring.

MUSHROOM GRAVY

Yield: 2 gallons

Ingredients

MUSHROOMS, FRESH	2 pounds
OR	
MUSHROOMS, CANNED, SLICED	2 1-pound cans
SALAD OIL	1/2 cup
BROWN SAUCE or PREPARED BEEF GRAVY	3 quarts
TOMATO SAUCE	2 quarts
INSTANT ONION POWDER	2 teaspoons
INSTANT GARLIC POWDER	1 teaspoon
SALT	as needed
BLACK PEPPER	as needed

Procedure

1. Rinse, pat dry, and slice fresh mushrooms (makes 2-1/2 quarts). Or, drain canned mushrooms.

2. Saute mushrooms in oil until golden.

3. Stir in remaining ingredients; heat thoroughly. Check seasoning, adding salt and pepper as needed.

MUSHROOM BROWN GRAVY

Yield: 1 gallon

Ingredients

MARGARINE	1/4 pound
BLACK PEPPER	1/2 teaspoon
ONION, cut into 1/4-inch dice	1 cup
MUSHROOMS, FRESH, 1/8-inch slices	1 pound
BROWN GRAVY*	1 gallon

Procedure

1. Heat margarine and pepper in heavy saucepan; add onion. Saute to golden brown.

2. Add mushrooms to onion; saute over high heat for 10 minutes, stirring frequently.

3. Add brown gravy to mixture; bring to a boil; simmer 10 minutes.

*BROWN GRAVY

Yield: 2 gallons

Ingredients

WATER	1 gallon
WATER, sufficient to equal	2 gallons
TOMATO PASTE	1/4 cup
SALT	1/4 cup
FAT from TOP of STOCK	1-1/2 cups
FLOUR, HARD WHEAT	1 quart

Procedure

1. Start with pan in which meat was roasted, containing drippings, crusted juices, and the sliced onion and carrots used to season the meat during roasting.

2. Set roast pan on top of range; simmer until juices and vegetables are dehydrated and quite dark brown in color.

3. Add 1 gallon of water; bring to a boil, stirring to dissolve brown particles. Boil 20 minutes.

4. Strain; measure; add water to equal required amount. Add tomato paste and salt, tasting to season correctly.

5. Bring to a boil; skim fat.

6. Evaporate moisture from fat. Add flour, making roux. Simmer 5 minutes.

7. Return stock to a boil. Add roux; whip smooth. Simmer 5 minutes. Check seasoning.

Barbecue Sauces

BARBECUE SAUCE

Yield: 1-1/2 gallons

Ingredients

BACON FAT	1/2 cup
ONION, finely minced	1 cup
WORCESTERSHIRE SAUCE	1/4 cup
PREPARED MUSTARD	3/4 cup
CATSUP	1 quart
VINEGAR	1/2 cup
SUGAR	1/2 cup
STOCK	2 quarts
HAM-STYLE SEASONING or SMOKE FLAVOR	2 ounces
BROWN GRAVY	2 quarts

Procedure

    1. Heat bacon fat; add onion; saute until golden brown.

    2. Add Worcestershire sauce; simmer 5 minutes.

    3. Add mustard, catsup, vinegar, sugar, stock, ham seasoning, and brown gravy.

    4. Bring to a boil; simmer 10 minutes.

BARBECUE SAUCE FOR CHICKEN

Yield: 1 gallon

Ingredients

ONION, chopped	3 cups
SALAD OIL or MARGARINE	1 cup (1/2 pound)
TOMATO SAUCE	1-1/2 quarts
WATER	2 cups
LEMON JUICE	1 cup
SUGAR, BROWN	1 cup (6 ounces)
WORCESTERSHIRE SAUCE	1 cup
PREPARED MUSTARD	1/2 cup
SALT	3 tablespoons
LIQUID HOT PEPPER SEASONING	1 teaspoon

Procedure

    1. Saute onion in salad oil or margarine until tender.

    2. Add remaining ingredients. Bring to a boil; simmer 15 minutes.

TURKEY BARBECUE SAUCE

Yield: 1 gallon

Ingredients

TOMATO SAUCE	1 No. 10 can
ORANGE MARMALADE	3 cups
SOY SAUCE	1-1/2 cups
DRY MUSTARD	1 tablespoon

Procedure

1. Combine all ingredients; mix well.
2. Simmer 30 minutes.
3. Use to baste turkeys during last hour of barbecuing. Serve remaining sauce over turkey portions.

FRESNO RAISIN BARBECUE SAUCE

Yield: 24 2-ounce portions

Ingredients

ONION, chopped	1 cup
CELERY, chopped	1-1/2 cups
GREEN PEPPER, chopped	1 cup
GARLIC, minced	3 cloves
OIL or DRIPPINGS	1/3 cup
TOMATO SAUCE	3 cups
WATER	1-1/2 cups
RAISINS, LIGHT or DARK	1-1/2 cups
CHILI POWDER	1-1/2 teaspoons
SALT	1/4 teaspoon

Procedure

1. Cook onion, celery, green pepper, and garlic slowly in oil until transparent.
2. Add remaining ingredients; simmer 15 to 20 minutes. Serve hot.

Hound Dog Roll with Cheese Garnish and Sauce

Durum-Macaroni HRI Program

HICKORY-SMOKED BARBECUE SAUCE

Yield: 1-1/4 gallons

Ingredients

ONION, finely chopped	1 pound
SALAD OIL	1/2 cup
VINEGAR	1 cup
TOMATO PUREE	1 quart
TOMATOES, CANNED	2 quarts
SYRUP, IMITATION MAPLE	2 cups
BEEF SOUP BASE	6 tablespoons
WORCESTERSHIRE SAUCE	1/3 cup
CHARCOAL or HICKORY SEASONING	4 teaspoons
LIQUID HOT PEPPER SEASONING	1/2 teaspoon
WATER	1 quart
GREEN PEPPER, chopped	1 cup

Procedure

1. Saute onion in oil until tender.

2. Add vinegar, tomato puree, tomatoes, syrup, beef soup base, Worcestershire sauce, seasonings, and water. Simmer, uncovered, 40 minutes.

3. Add chopped green pepper; simmer 5 minutes longer.

Note

For a thicker sauce, combine 2 ounces (1/2 cup) flour with enough water to make a thin smooth paste. Stir into sauce; simmer until slightly thickened.

WINE BARBECUE SAUCE

Yield: 1-3/4 quarts

Ingredients

ONION, chopped	8 ounces
BUTTER	2 ounces
WHITE DINNER WINE	2 cups
OREGANO	1 teaspoon
CUMIN	2 tablespoons
CATSUP	1/2 cup
BLACK PEPPER	1/2 teaspoon
SUGAR, BROWN	1 tablespoon
TOMATOES, CANNED, broken up	3-1/2 cups
SALT	as needed
CORNSTARCH	3 tablespoons
WATER	1/2 cup
	(approximately)

Procedure

1. Saute onion in butter until wilted. Add wine, herbs, catsup, pepper, brown sugar, and tomatoes.

2. Bring mixture to a boil; cook slowly for 20 minutes. Add salt to taste.

3. Blend cornstarch with enough cold water to make a smooth paste. Add to hot sauce; cook and stir until clear. (For vegetables, such as green beans, corn and lima beans, or zucchini, use one part sauce to two parts vegetables.)

Butters

MAITRE D'HOTEL BUTTER

Yield: 48 portions

Ingredients

PARSLEY FLAKES	1 cup
LEMON JUICE	3 tablespoons
SALT	2 teaspoons
WHITE PEPPER	1 teaspoon
BUTTER	2 pounds

Procedure

1. Mix parsley flakes and lemon juice; let stand 10 minutes for parsley to soften.

2. Combine softened parsley flakes with salt and white pepper.

3. Beat butter until creamy; add parsley mixture gradually, mixing thoroughly.

4. Shape into rolls on waxed paper. Refrigerate until firm. Slice as needed.

5. Use on grilled steaks, chops, poultry, and fish.

PAPRIKA BUTTER
(for broiling chicken)

Yield: for 48 portions

Ingredients

BUTTER or MARGARINE, melted	2 pounds
PAPRIKA	1/2 cup
LEMON JUICE	3 tablespoons
INSTANT ONION POWDER	2 teaspoons
SALT	2 teaspoons
WHITE PEPPER	2 teaspoons

Procedure

1. Combine all ingredients; mix thoroughly.

2. Brush mixture on chicken for broiling.

ONION BUTTER

Yield: 2 pounds, 6 ounces

Ingredients

BUTTER or MARGARINE	2 pounds
ONION SOUP MIX	6 ounces

Procedure
1. Beat butter to soften.
2. Gradually add dry onion soup mix; blend thoroughly.
3. Store, covered, in refrigerator.
4. Use on hamburgers, broiled steak, chops, or fish.

MUSHROOM-BUTTER SAUCE

Yield: 8 portions

Ingredients

BUTTER	8 ounces
MUSHROOMS, SLICED, drained	1 8-ounce can
LEMON JUICE	1/4 cup
SALT	1 teaspoon

Procedure
1. Melt butter. Add mushrooms, lemon juice, and salt.
2. Heat. Serve over broiled or panfried trout.

ROQUEFORT BUTTER

Yield: 6 pounds

Ingredients

BUTTER	4 pounds
CHEESE, ROQUEFORT, crumbled	2 pounds
SALT	2 tablespoons
WHITE PEPPER	1 tablespoon

Procedure
1. Whip butter until soft and fluffy.
2. Gradually beat in cheese, salt, and white pepper.
3. Store, covered, in refrigerator.
4. Use for broiled chicken, hamburgers, lamb chops, steaks, fish steaks, shrimp, etc., putting a small amount on food during last 1 or 2 minutes of broiling. Or, use butter to top cooked vegetables, such as broccoli, cauliflower, peas, asparagus, or green beans.

LEMON-GARLIC BUTTER

Yield: 1 pound

Ingredients

BUTTER	1 pound
LEMON PEEL, grated	1 tablespoon
PAPRIKA	1 tablespoon
LEMON JUICE, fresh	1/2 cup
GARLIC, crushed	1 clove

Procedure

1. Cream butter on mixer, using paddle attachment. Add grated lemon peel and paprika.

2. Gradually add lemon juice, continuing to mix until all liquid is absorbed. Add juice from crushed garlic; mix well.

3. Form mixture into sticks or blocks; chill until firm.

4. Slice into pats for serving on broiled steaks. Or, use as a spread for garlic toast.

LEMON-CURRY BUTTER

Yield: 1 pound

Ingredients

BUTTER	1 pound
LEMON PEEL, grated	2 tablespoons
CURRY POWDER	1 teaspoon
LEMON JUICE, fresh	1/3 cup
SOY SAUCE	1 tablespoon

Procedure

1. Cream butter in mixer, using paddle attachment. Add grated lemon peel and curry powder.

2. Gradually add lemon juice and soy sauce, continuing to mix until liquid is absorbed.

3. Form mixture into sticks or blocks; chill until firm.

4. Slice into pats for use on broiled lamb chops, chicken, shrimp, or steamed rice.

SEASONED LEMON BUTTER

Yield: 1 pound

Ingredients

BUTTER	1 pound
LEMON PEEL, grated	1 to 2 tablespoons
WORCESTERSHIRE SAUCE	1 tablespoon
LEMON JUICE, fresh	1/3 cup

Procedure

1. Cream butter on mixer, using paddle attachment. Add grated lemon peel.

2. Gradually add Worcestershire sauce and lemon juice, continuing to mix until all liquid is absorbed.

3. Form mixture into sticks or blocks; chill until firm.

4. Slice into pats to serve on broiled fish or lobster or on baked potatoes.

LIME BUTTER FISH SAUCE

Yield: 2-3/4 cups

Ingredients

BUTTER	1 pound
LIME JUICE	3/4 cup
LIQUID HOT PEPPER SEASONING	1 teaspoon

Procedure

Melt butter; add lime juice and liquid hot pepper seasoning.

LEMON OR ORANGE MINT BUTTER FOR PEAS

Yield: 1 pound

Ingredients

BUTTER, softened	1 pound
LEMON JUICE	1/4 cup
LEMON or ORANGE PEEL, grated	1 teaspoon
MINT, FRESH, chopped	1/2 to 3/4 cup

Procedure

1. Cream butter with lemon juice and grated peel. Add mint.

2. Refrigerate until needed.

3. Use to butter (and season) hot, cooked peas.

DRAWN BUTTER-EGG SAUCE

Yield: 2 quarts

Ingredients

BUTTER	1/4 pound
FLOUR	3/4 cup
SALT	1-1/2 teaspoons
WHITE PEPPER	1/2 teaspoon
WATER, boiling	1-1/2 quarts
LEMON JUICE	1-1/2 tablespoons
BUTTER	1/4 pound
EGGS, hard-cooked, finely chopped	8
PARSLEY, chopped (optional)	1/4 cup

Procedure

1. Melt first amount of butter; blend in flour, salt, and white pepper.

2. Add boiling water, stirring until thickened and smooth. Simmer, stirring occasionally, for about 5 minutes.

3. Add lemon juice. Stir in second amount of butter, adding a little at a time.

4. Add eggs and the parsley, if desired. Serve with poached or baked trout.

HERBED LEMON BUTTER

Yield: 1 pound

Ingredients

BUTTER	1 pound
LEMON PEEL, grated	2 tablespoons
OREGANO, crushed	1/2 teaspoon
ROSEMARY, crushed	1/2 teaspoon
THYME, crushed	1/2 teaspoon
LEMON JUICE, fresh	1/3 cup

Procedure

1. Cream butter on mixer, using paddle attachment. Add grated lemon peel and herbs.

2. Gradually add lemon juice, continuing to mix until all liquid is absorbed.

3. Form mixture into sticks or blocks; chill until firm. Slice into pats for serving on broiled fish, baked potatoes, or hot biscuits.

White Sauce Family

QUICK-METHOD WHITE SAUCE

Yield: approximately 1 gallon

Ingredients

WATER	1 gallon
BUTTER, MARGARINE, or SHORTENING	1 pound
NONFAT DRY MILK	1-1/2 pounds
FLOUR	2 cups (8 ounces)
SALT	2 tablespoons
WHITE PEPPER	1 teaspoon
WATER, cold	3 cups

Procedure

1. Heat water to boiling. Stir in butter. Stir in nonfat dry milk.

2. Combine flour, salt, and pepper; blend with 3 cups cold water to make a smooth paste.

3. Using a wire whip, stir flour mixture into hot liquid. Cook and stir over low heat until thick and smooth.

Variations

(Based on 3 quarts white sauce)

Mustard Sauce Add 3/4 to 1 cup prepared mustard. Blend and heat.

Mushroom Sauce Add 1 quart thinly sliced, sauteed mushrooms. Heat.

Coral Sauce Add 1-1/2 cups tomato puree and 1 large onion, grated. Blend and heat.

Caper Sauce Add 1-1/4 to 1-1/2 cups capers, whole or chopped. Stir in 1/4 cup lemon juice, if desired.

Hot Tartar Sauce Add 1 cup chopped sweet pickles or sweet pickle relish, drained; 1 cup onion, finely chopped; 1 cup parsley, chopped; 3/4 cup pimiento-stuffed olives, chopped, and 1 quart heavy mayonnaise. Blend; heat gently.

Horseradish Sauce Add 1-1/4 to 1-1/2 cups drained horseradish. Add salt and pepper to taste. For a richer sauce, use 1-1/2 cups drained horseradish and fold in 1 cup cream, whipped.

Rice with Sour Cream Dressing and Chive Garnish

Rice Council

BASIC CHEDDAR CHEESE SAUCE

Yield: 1-1/8 gallons

Ingredients

BUTTER	1 pound, 2 ounces
FLOUR	12 ounces
SALT	1 tablespoon
PAPRIKA	1 tablespoon
WHITE PEPPER	3/4 teaspoon
MILK, scalded	3 quarts
CHEESE, AGED CHEDDAR, shredded	2-1/4 pounds

Procedure

1. Melt butter in heavy saucepot or steam-jacketed kettle; blend in flour and seasonings. Simmer, stirring constantly with a wire whip, for about 5 minutes.

2. Add hot milk gradually; stir and cook until thickened and no starch flavor remains, about 15 minutes.

3. Remove from heat; stir in cheese, stirring until cheese melts and sauce is smooth.

Note

To store, cover closely; refrigerate.

CHEDDAR CHEESE SAUCE FOR MEATS

Yield: approximately 1 gallon

Ingredients

BASIC CHEDDAR CHEESE SAUCE*	3 quarts
MILK	3 cups
CHEESE, BLUE, crumbled	6 ounces
BACON, cooked, diced	6 ounces
WORCESTERSHIRE SAUCE	3 ounces

Procedure

1. Blend Basic Cheddar Cheese Sauce, milk, and blue cheese over moderate heat. Stir in bacon and Worcestershire sauce.

2. Ladle hot sauce over chopped sirloin patties, Salisbury steak, lamb chops, or veal cutlets just before serving.

*See recipe, above.

CHEESE SAUCE FOR VEGETABLES

Yield: approximately 1-1/8 gallons

Ingredients

BASIC CHEDDAR CHEESE SAUCE*	3 quarts
MILK or DRAINED VEGETABLE LIQUID	3 cups
MUSHROOMS, sliced, cooked	3 cups
PIMIENTO, chopped	9 ounces

Procedure

1. Blend Basic Cheddar Cheese Sauce and milk over moderate heat; stir in mushrooms and pimiento.

2. Ladle over individual portions of broccoli, brussels sprouts, whole green beans, cauliflower, spinach, or cabbage just before serving.

*See recipe, facing page.

CHEDDAR CHEESE SAUCE FOR FISH

Yield: approximately 1 gallon

Ingredients

BASIC CHEDDAR CHEESE SAUCE*	3 quarts
MILK	3 cups
SWEET PICKLE RELISH, drained	3 cups
CELERY SEED	1 tablespoon
LIQUID HOT PEPPER SEASONING	2 to 3 teaspoons

Procedure

1. Blend Basic Cheddar Cheese Sauce and milk over moderate heat; stir in pickle relish, celery seed, and liquid hot pepper seasoning.

2. Ladle over portions of baked or broiled cod, haddock, halibut, perch, or whitefish or over poached flounder or sole.

*See recipe, facing page.

CHEESE SAUCE

Yield: 2 quarts

Ingredients

BUTTER or MARGARINE	1 cup
FLOUR	1 cup
DRY MUSTARD	1 tablespoon
SALT	1 teaspoon
WORCESTERSHIRE SAUCE	2 tablespoons
MILK	2 quarts
CHEESE, SHARP CHEDDAR, shredded	1 pound

Procedure

1. Make white sauce of butter, flour, seasonings, and milk.

2. When thickened and smooth, add cheese. Stir until cheese is melted.

ROQUEFORT SAUCE BASE

Yield: 1-1/2 pounds (enough for 1 gallon sauce)

Ingredients

CHEESE, ROQUEFORT	1/2 pound
BUTTER or MARGARINE	1/2 pound
FLOUR, ALL-PURPOSE	1/2 pound

Procedure

1. Mash Roquefort cheese with butter; gradually blend in flour.

2. Store, refrigerated, in a covered container.

3. *To make sauce,* add to hot milk in the proportion of 1-1/2 ounces sauce base to 1 cup milk. Stir over medium heat until sauce bubbles and thickens. Season to taste with salt, pepper, and cayenne pepper *or* paprika.

4. Use sauce with fish, poultry, baked potatoes, vegetables, eggs, or pasta.

Note

Vary sauce as desired with grated onion, chopped parsley, chopped chives, chopped nuts, sieved hard-cooked egg yolk, drained pickle relish, capers, crumbled herbs, chopped green or ripe olives, minced ham or chicken, crumbled crisp bacon, etc.

SAN JOAQUIN SAUCE

Yield: approximately 2 quarts

Ingredients

OLIVES, RIPE, PITTED	2 cups
WHITE SAUCE, MEDIUM	1-1/2 quarts
WORCESTERSHIRE SAUCE	1 tablespoon
PARSLEY, finely chopped	1/3 cup
CAYENNE PEPPER	1/8 teaspoon
EGGS, hard-cooked, chopped	6
SALT	as needed

Procedure

1. Cut olives into large pieces.

2. Combine white sauce with Worcestershire sauce, parsley, and cayenne pepper. Add eggs and olives. Season with salt to taste.

3. Serve hot over cooked asparagus, broccoli, or cauliflower.

SORCERY SAUCE

Yield: 2 gallons

Ingredients

SHORTENING	1-3/4 pounds
FLOUR	1 quart
CHICKEN SOUP BASE	1 cup (8 ounces)
WHITE PEPPER	2 teaspoons
ONION, grated	1/4 cup
WATER	1-3/4 gallons
SOUR CREAM	2 quarts

Procedure

1. Melt shortening. Stir in flour and soup base. Cook, stirring, over low heat until well blended. Add white pepper, onion, and water. Cook and stir until thickened.

2. Remove from heat. Stir in sour cream. Serve over cooked chicken, meat, or fish.

MORNAY SAUCE

Yield: approximately 3-1/4 quarts

Ingredients

BUTTER	8 ounces
FLOUR	2 cups (8 ounces)
MILK, hot	2-1/2 quarts
SALT	1 tablespoon
NUTMEG	1/4 teaspoon
CREAM	2 cups
EGG YOLKS	6
WORCESTERSHIRE SAUCE	1 tablespoon
CHEESE, SWISS, grated	3 ounces
CHEESE, PARMESAN, grated	3 ounces

Procedure

1. Melt butter in heavy saucepan; blend in flour. Add hot milk, beating briskly with wire whip. Cook, stirring, until thickened and smooth. Season with salt and nutmeg.

2. Stir in cream. Heat; simmer a few minutes.

3. Beat egg yolks; add Worcestershire sauce and grated cheeses. Add a small amount of the hot mixture; blend.

4. Gradually add egg mixture to hot (not boiling) sauce, stirring constantly. Remove from heat.

Note

Fold in a small amount of unsweetened whipped cream, if desired, when using sauce for topping a dish to be browned.

MARGUERY SAUCE
(for poached fillets of fish)

Yield: 2 quarts

Ingredients

BUTTER or MARGARINE	1/2 pound
MUSHROOMS, chopped	2 cups
FLOUR	1/2 cup
CAYENNE PEPPER	dash
FISH STOCK	3 cups
OYSTERS	12
SHRIMP	12
EGG YOLKS	8
CREAM	2 cups
LEMON JUICE	1/2 cup
CAPERS	2 tablespoons

Procedure

1. Melt butter; add mushrooms; simmer for 5 minutes.

2. Add flour and cayenne pepper; stir until well blended. Remove from heat.

3. Gradually stir in fish stock; return to heat. Cook over low heat, stirring constantly until thickened and smooth.

4. Chop soft portions of oysters and shrimp; add to sauce.

5. Beat egg yolks slightly; add cream and a little of the hot sauce. Stir gradually into remaining sauce.

6. Gradually add lemon juice, stirring over low heat until thoroughly heated. Add capers; correct seasoning.

SPECIAL SAUCE

Yield: approximately 3 quarts

Ingredients

ONION, chopped	2/3 cup
GREEN PEPPER, chopped	1/3 cup
BUTTER or MARGARINE	1 cup
FLOUR	2/3 cup
SALT	1 tablespoon
GARLIC SALT	1/4 teaspoon
PIMIENTO, chopped	1/3 cup
MILK, hot	2-1/2 quarts
EGGS, beaten	5

Procedure

1. Saute onion and green pepper in butter. Add flour. Stir until bubbly. Add seasonings, pimiento, and hot milk. Cook, stirring constantly, until mixture boils. Cook 5 minutes.

2. Add a little of the hot sauce to beaten eggs. Gradually add egg mixture to sauce. Stir. Cook 10 minutes. The sauce should be fluffy.

DILL SAUCE FOR MEAT AND FISH

Yield: approximately 3 quarts

Ingredients

SHORTENING	1-1/2 cups (10-1/2 ounces)
DILL POWDER	1 tablespoon
PARSLEY, chopped	3 tablespoons
ONION SOUP BASE	1 8-ounce jar
FLOUR	1-1/4 cups (5 ounces)
WATER	1-1/2 quarts
SOUR CREAM	1-1/2 quarts
DRY WHITE WINE (optional)	2 tablespoons

Procedure

1. Melt shortening. Stir in seasonings, onion soup base, and flour. Add water; cook, stirring, 3 minutes, until mixture is slightly thickened.

2. Stir in sour cream; heat just to boiling point. Add wine, if desired. Serve over beef or seafood.

Note

If fresh dill is available, omit dill powder and parsley. Add 1 cup finely chopped dill.

Mayonnaise – Sour Cream Sauces

SATIN SAUCE

Yield: 1 quart

Ingredients

EGG YOLKS, beaten	12 (1 cup)
CREAM, LIGHT	2-2/3 cups
SALT	2 teaspoons
NUTMEG	1/2 teaspoon
CAYENNE PEPPER	1/8 teaspoon
LEMON JUICE	1/4 cup
BUTTER or MARGARINE, softened	3/4 cup (6 ounces)

Procedure

1. Combine all ingredients except butter.
2. Cook over low heat or in a double boiler, stirring constantly until mixture thickens.
3. Remove from heat; blend in butter. Serve on cooked celery, broccoli, or zucchini.

GLORIETTA SAUCE

Yield: 2 quarts

Ingredients

ALMONDS, CHOPPED, toasted	1-1/2 cups
MAYONNAISE	1-1/2 quarts
DILL PICKLE, chopped	1 cup
PARSLEY, finely chopped	3/4 cup
ONION, finely chopped	1/2 cup
PREPARED HORSERADISH	2 tablespoons
PIMIENTO, chopped	1/3 cup

Procedure

1. Combine all ingredients.
2. Serve over hot cooked asparagus, broccoli, or green beans.

LIME HOLLANDAISE SAUCE

Yield: 2 cups

Ingredients

EGG YOLKS	8
SALT	1 teaspoon
DRY MUSTARD	1 teaspoon
SUGAR	1 teaspoon
LIQUID HOT PEPPER SEASONING	1/2 teaspoon
BUTTER, melted	2 cups (1 pound)
LIME JUICE	1/2 cup

Procedure

1. Beat egg yolks until thick and lemon-colored; add salt, mustard, sugar, and liquid hot pepper seasoning.
2. Beating constantly, add 1 cup of the melted butter, a small amount at a time.
3. Combine remaining melted butter with lime juice. Add to egg yolk mixture a small amount at a time, beating constantly.
4. Serve with broccoli, asparagus, broiled fish, or poached salmon or flounder.

GREEN GODDESS FISH SAUCE

Yield: 2-1/4 quarts

Ingredients

GARLIC CLOVES	2
SALT	1 teaspoon
ANCHOVY PASTE	3/4 cup
TARRAGON WINE VINEGAR	1 cup
MAYONNAISE	5-1/2 cups
SOUR CREAM	2 cups
PARSLEY, chopped	2 cups
CHIVES, DEHYDRATED or FREEZE-DRIED	1 cup

Procedure

1. Crush garlic cloves with salt.
2. Combine with anchovy paste and vinegar.
3. Combine mayonnaise and sour cream; blend in vinegar mixture. Stir in parsley and chives. Chill.

MOCK HOLLANDAISE SAUCE

Yield: 1 gallon

Ingredients

BUTTER or MARGARINE	8 ounces
FLOUR	4 ounces
MILK	2 quarts
SALT	2 teaspoons
WHITE PEPPER	1 teaspoon
CAYENNE PEPPER	1/4 teaspoon
SUGAR	4 tablespoons
EGG YOLKS, beaten	1 cup
LEMON JUICE	2 cups
MAYONNAISE	1 quart

Procedure

1. Melt butter; add flour; blend.
2. Add milk; cook, stirring, until thickened. Season with salt, white pepper, cayenne pepper, and sugar.
3. Add a little of the hot mixture to the beaten egg yolks; blend. Gradually add to remaining hot mixture, stirring constantly. Cook for 2 minutes; remove from heat.
4. Add the lemon juice and mayonnaise. Blend.

CHIVE-SOUR CREAM SAUCE

Yield: 1-1/2 quarts

Ingredients

SOUR CREAM	1 quart
MAYONNAISE	2 cups
LEMON JUICE, fresh	1/4 cup
ONION SALT	2 teaspoons
CHIVES, DEHYDRATED or FREEZE-DRIED	1 cup

Procedure

1. Combine all ingredients; mix until blended.
2. Garnish with additional chives, if desired.
3. Serve with cold poached salmon or other fish, with vegetables, aspics or as a topping for jellied madrilene.

Avocado with Grapes a la Russe

California Table Grape Commission

Casserole Sandwiches

Spanish Green Olive Commission
California Apricot Advisory Board

TARRAGON SAUCE

Yield: approximately 1 quart

Ingredients

MAYONNAISE	2 cups
SOUR CREAM	2 cups
PREPARED MUSTARD	1/4 cup
TARRAGON, DRY, finely crumbled	1 teaspoon

Procedure
1. Combine all ingredients, blending well.
2. Serve over hot or chilled, drained green beans.

ONION-SOUR CREAM SAUCE

Yield: 1 quart

Ingredients

SOUR CREAM	1 quart
INSTANT CHOPPED ONION	4 teaspoons
PAPRIKA	4 teaspoons
SALT	1/2 teaspoon
BLACK PEPPER	1/4 teaspoon
LEMON JUICE, fresh	2 tablespoons

Procedure
1. Combine all ingredients. Heat gently but thoroughly. *Do not boil.*
2. Serve, hot or cold, over vegetables.

HORSERADISH SAUCE

Yield: 1 quart

Ingredients

SOUR CREAM	1 quart
HORSERADISH	2/3 to 3/4 cup
SALT	2 teaspoons
SUGAR	3 tablespoons

Procedure
1. Combine all ingredients. Chill.
2. Serve with ham, tongue, boiled beef, cold cuts, or tomato aspic.

Beef Sandwich with Mayonnaise Sauce

National Sandwich Idea Contest

COLD VERTE SAUCE

Yield: 1-1/4 quarts

Ingredients

MAYONNAISE	1-1/4 quarts
CHIVES, chopped	1/2 cup
TARRAGON, DRY	1 tablespoon
PARSLEY, chopped	1/2 cup
DILL WEED	1 tablespoon
LEMON JUICE	2 tablespoons

Procedure
1. Combine all ingredients; chill.
2. Serve with breaded fish portions or cold poached salmon.

CUCUMBER SAUCE

Yield: 100 portions, approximately 1 ounce each

Ingredients

CUCUMBERS, finely diced, drained	2 quarts
MAYONNAISE	1-1/2 quarts
SOUR CREAM	1 quart
SALT	1-1/2 tablespoons
WHITE PEPPER	1 teaspoon
PAPRIKA	1 tablespoon
LEMON JUICE	1/2 cup
ONION, grated	2 tablespoons

Procedure

1. Combine all ingredients; mix well. Chill.
2. Serve with cold poached salmon.

GOURMET FISH SAUCE

Yield: approximately 5 quarts

Ingredients

SOUR CREAM	2-1/2 quarts
CUCUMBERS, peeled, seeded, coarsely grated	2 quarts
ONION, finely chopped	1-1/2 cups
LEMON JUICE	1/4 cup
PREPARED HORSERADISH	1/3 cup
SALT	1 tablespoon
BLACK PEPPER	1/2 teaspoon
PAPRIKA	1 teaspoon

Procedure

1. Combine all ingredients, mixing gently.
2. Chill for several hours. Serve with fried, baked, or broiled trout or with chilled trout in aspic.

LAMAZE SAUCE
(for fish)

Yield: 100 portions, approximately 2 ounces each

Ingredients

MAYONNAISE or SALAD DRESSING	1 gallon
CATSUP	1 quart
PICKLE RELISH	1 quart
EGGS, hard-cooked, finely chopped	12

Procedure

Combine all ingredients; mix well. Chill.

CUCUMBER-SOUR CREAM SAUCE

Yield: 1-1/4 quarts

Ingredients

SOUR CREAM	2 cups
CUCUMBERS, finely chopped, drained	3 cups
VINEGAR	2-1/2 tablespoons
SUGAR	4 teaspoons
DILL SEED	1/2 teaspoon
WHITE PEPPER	1/8 teaspoon

Procedure

1. Combine all ingredients.

2. Refrigerate at least 1 hour for flavors to blend. Serve over broiled or baked fish, fish mousse, or potato salad.

FISHERMAN'S WHARF ALMONDAISE SAUCE

Yield: approximately 2-1/4 quarts

Ingredients

CREAM CHEESE	2 pounds
BUTTER or MARGARINE	8 ounces
MILK	2 cups
EGGS, beaten	4
LEMON JUICE	3/4 cup
CAYENNE PEPPER	1/4 teaspoon
ALMONDS, DICED, ROASTED	1-1/2 cups

Procedure

1. Soften cream cheese and butter in top of double boiler or in steam-jacketed kettle.

2. Blend in milk. (Mixture becomes thin but thickens again with addition of eggs and lemon juice.)

3. Stir in eggs; heat through. Blend in lemon juice and cayenne pepper.

4. Just before serving, stir in almonds, reserving a small amount for garnish.

5. Use as a base for seafood dishes of shrimp, crab, or lobster. Or, serve over broccoli, asparagus, green beans, or brussels sprouts. Garnish with reserved almonds.

Tomato Sauces

CREOLE SAUCE

Yield: 2-1/2 quarts; 25 2-1/2-ounce portions

Ingredients

HAM or BACON FAT	1/2 cup
BLACK PEPPER	1 teaspoon
CELERY, cut into 3/8-inch dice	1 quart
ONION, cut into 3/8-inch dice	3/4 quart
GARLIC, crushed	1 clove
TOMATO PASTE	2 cups
OR	
TOMATO PUREE	3 cups
TOMATOES	1/2 No. 10 can
BAY LEAF	1
OREGANO, FLAKED	1 teaspoon
SALT	2 teaspoons
PAPRIKA	2 teaspoons
SUGAR	4-1/2 ounces
GREEN PEPPER, cut into 3/8-inch dice	1 cup

Procedure

1. Heat fat with pepper in heavy bottomed pan. Add celery, onion, and garlic; saute to a golden brown over high heat, turning frequently.

2. Add remaining ingredients; bring to a boil. Lower heat; simmer gently for 1 hour.

CREOLE RICE SAUCE FOR OMELETS

Yield: 3 quarts

Ingredients

INSTANT ONION FLAKES, reconstituted	1/2 cup
INSTANT GREEN PEPPER FLAKES, reconstituted	1/2 cup
BUTTER or MARGARINE	4 ounces
TOMATO SAUCE WITH MUSHROOMS	1 quart
WATER	2 cups
SALT	1 teaspoon
OREGANO	1/2 teaspoon
BLACK PEPPER	1/2 teaspoon
RICE, cooked, hot	1-1/2 quarts
OLIVES, GREEN, PIMIENTO-STUFFED, sliced	1 cup
OMELETS, unfolded	24
CHEESE, AMERICAN or SWISS, grated	1-1/2 pounds

Procedure

1. Combine onion, green pepper, butter, tomato sauce, water, and seasonings; simmer for 15 minutes. Stir in rice and olives.

2. Spoon 1/2 cup sauce over each unfolded omelet. Sprinkle with cheese. Run under broiler until cheese melts.

CREOLE TOMATO SAUCE

Yield: approximately 3-1/4 gallons

Ingredients

TOMATOES, broken up	2 No. 10 cans
CATSUP	1 No. 10 can
WATER	3 quarts
SUGAR	1/2 cup
WHITE PEPPER	1/2 teaspoon
SALT	as needed
CORNSTARCH	2 cups
WATER, cold	1 quart

Procedure

1. Combine tomatoes, catsup, first amount of water, sugar, and white pepper. Bring to a boil; reduce heat; simmer 10 to 15 minutes. Add salt to taste.

2. Blend cornstarch and cold water to form a thin paste. Add to sauce. Cook, stirring, until sauce is clear and thickened.

ITALIAN TOMATO SAUCE

Yield: 1 gallon

Ingredients

TOMATO PUREE	1-1/2 quarts
TOMATO PASTE	1 quart
WATER	1-1/2 quarts
COOKING OIL	1/2 cup
SUGAR	3 tablespoons
ITALIAN SEASONING	3 tablespoons
INSTANT ONION POWDER	3 tablespoons
INSTANT MINCED GARLIC	2 teaspoons
SALT	2 teaspoons
BLACK PEPPER	1 teaspoon

Procedure

1. Combine tomato puree, tomato paste, and water; mix. Bring to a boil; stir in oil.

2. Add remaining ingredients. Simmer 12 to 15 minutes, stirring occasionally.

TOMATO SAUCE

Yield: 50 1-1/2-ounce portions

Ingredients

TOMATOES, CANNED	3-1/2 quarts
ONION, sliced	1-1/2 cups
SALT	1 tablespoon
SUGAR	1 tablespoon
CELERY SALT	2 teaspoons
BLACK PEPPER	1-1/2 teaspoons
BAY LEAF	1
MARGARINE	1/2 pound
FLOUR	1-1/8 cups
	(4-1/2 ounces)

Procedure

1. Combine tomatoes, onion, salt, sugar, celery salt, pepper, and bay leaf; cook 10 minutes. Remove bay leaf; force mixture through a sieve.

2. Melt margarine; blend in the flour. Gradually add the strained tomato mixture; cook, stirring, until sauce is thickened.

OLIVE-TOMATO SAUCE

Yield: 1 quart

Ingredients

OLIVES, RIPE, CHOPPED	2 cups
TOMATOES, CANNED	1 quart
INSTANT MINCED ONION	2 tablespoons
PARSLEY, chopped	1/4 cup
VINEGAR	2 tablespoons
SUGAR	2 tablespoons
SWEET BASIL	1 teaspoon
THYME	1/2 teaspoon
GARLIC SALT	1 teaspoon
CORNSTARCH	2 tablespoons
WATER	2 tablespoons

Procedure

1. Combine olives, tomatoes, and seasonings. Bring to a boil; reduce heat; simmer 15 minutes.

2. Blend cornstarch and water. Stir into sauce; cook, stirring, until sauce thickens. Serve hot or cold with fish sticks or hamburgers.

MEAT SAUCE

Yield: 30 portions

Ingredients

COOKING OIL	2 to 4 ounces
GROUND BEEF	6 pounds
SPAGHETTI SAUCE MIX	8 ounces
ONION, chopped	5 ounces
GREEN PEPPER, chopped	5 ounces
CATSUP	2 quarts
WATER	2 quarts

Procedure

1. Heat cooking oil; add ground beef. Cook for 15 minutes, stirring to break up meat.

2. Add remaining ingredients. Cook slowly 1 hour.

MUSHROOM SPAGHETTI SAUCE

Yield: 2-1/4 gallons; 50 portions, approximately 3/4 cup each

Ingredients

SHORTENING or SALAD OIL	3 cups
ONION, chopped	2-1/4 quarts
PARSLEY FLAKES	1 cup
GARLIC, minced	3 tablespoons
MUSHROOMS, CANNED, STEMS AND PIECES, drained	4-1/2 quarts
MUSHROOM LIQUID	2-1/4 quarts
TOMATOES	3/4 No. 10 can (2-1/4 quarts)
TOMATO PUREE	3 No. 10 cans
SALT	1/2 cup
CAYENNE PEPPER	1-1/2 teaspoons
SUGAR	1 cup

Procedure

1. Melt shortening in heavy skillet. Add onion, parsley flakes, garlic, and drained mushrooms; saute until lightly browned.

2. Add mushroom liquid, tomatoes, tomato puree, and seasonings. Bring to a boil; reduce heat and simmer slowly about 2 hours, stirring occasionally, until sauce is thickened.

RAISIN-GROUND BEEF SAUCE

Yield: 100 1/2-cup portions

Ingredients

ONION, chopped	2-1/2 pounds
CELERY, chopped	2-1/2 pounds
SHORTENING	1 pound
GROUND BEEF	17 pounds
RAISINS, SEEDLESS	4 pounds, 6 ounces
TOMATO PUREE	3-1/2 quarts
WATER	3 quarts
SALT	1/2 cup
WORCESTERSHIRE SAUCE	2 tablespoons
CHILI POWDER	2 tablespoons
PAPRIKA	2 teaspoons

Procedure

1. Saute onion and celery in shortening until tender but not brown.

2. Add beef; brown, stirring constantly. Add remaining ingredients; simmer 20 to 25 minutes until ingredients are well blended.

3. Serve over cooked spaghetti, noodles, or macaroni.

SPANISH SAUCE

Yield: 3 quarts

Ingredients

ONION, sliced	2 cups (7 ounces)
GREEN PEPPER, cut into strips	1 cup (6 ounces)
BUTTER or MARGARINE	12 ounces
SALT	1-1/2 tablespoons
SUGAR	1/4 cup
CAYENNE PEPPER	3/8 teaspoon
MUSHROOMS, CANNED, SLICED	1 cup
TOMATOES, CANNED	2-1/4 quarts
TAPIOCA, QUICK-COOKING	3 tablespoons

Procedure

1. Saute onion and green pepper strips in butter until tender but not brown.

2. Add remaining ingredients. Cover; simmer about 15 minutes, stirring occasionally.

Soup – Based Sauces

A LA KING SAUCE

Yield: 1 gallon

Ingredients

GREEN PEPPER, chopped	2 cups
MUSHROOMS, sliced	12 ounces
BUTTER or MARGARINE	2 ounces
MILK	1 quart
CREAM OF CHICKEN SOUP, CONDENSED	1 50-ounce can
PIMIENTO, chopped	1/4 cup
SALT	1 teaspoon
WATER	2 cups
FLOUR	1-1/2 cups

Procedure

1. Cook green pepper and mushrooms in butter until tender.

2. Blend milk with soup; stir into cooked vegetables. Add pimiento and salt; heat.

3. Blend water with flour; stir into hot soup mixture. Cook, stirring, until thickened. Adjust for salt, if necessary.

4. Serve with baked or fried breaded fish or with chicken, omelets, scrambled eggs, etc.

HORSERADISH SAUCE

Yield: 1-1/2 quarts

Ingredients

TOMATO SOUP, CONDENSED	1 50-ounce can
PREPARED MUSTARD	1/4 cup
HORSERADISH	1/4 cup
CLOVES, GROUND	dash

Procedure

1. Combine all ingredients; blend.

2. Heat slowly to blend flavors. Serve on cooked beef, pork, ham, or meat loaf.

HOT VERTE SAUCE

Yield: approximately 2-3/4 quarts

Ingredients

CREAM OF CELERY or CREAM OF MUSHROOM SOUP, CONDENSED	1 50-ounce can
MILK	3-1/2 cups
ONION, grated	1 cup
LEMON JUICE	1/3 cup
SPINACH, cooked, finely chopped	1-1/2 cups

Procedure

Combine soup and milk. Add onion, lemon juice, and spinach; heat thoroughly.

MUSHROOM AMANDINE SAUCE

Yield: 1-3/4 quarts

Ingredients

ALMONDS, SLIVERED	1 cup
BUTTER or MARGARINE	2 ounces
CREAM OF MUSHROOM SOUP, CONDENSED	1 50-ounce can
WATER	1-1/2 cups
ONION, finely chopped	1/4 cup
SHERRY	1/4 cup

Procedure

1. Stirring constantly, saute almonds in butter until lightly browned.
2. Blend in soup, water, and onion; heat slowly. *Do not boil.*
3. Stir in sherry before serving over broiled or baked trout.

SAUCE INDIA

Yield: 2 quarts

Ingredients

ONION, finely chopped	1-1/2 cups
BUTTER or MARGARINE	2 ounces
CURRY POWDER	4 teaspoons
CHUTNEY, chopped	1/2 to 3/4 cup
TOMATO SOUP, CONDENSED	1 50-ounce can
WATER	1 cup

Procedure

1. Saute onion in butter until softened and transparent.
2. Blend in curry powder.
3. Add remaining ingredients; bring to a boil, stirring occasionally. Simmer 5 minutes to blend flavors.
4. Serve over cooked veal, beef, pork, or chicken.

OLIVE-MUSHROOM SAUCE

Yield: approximately 3 quarts

Ingredients

CREAM OF MUSHROOM SOUP, CONDENSED	1 50-ounce can
OLIVES, PIMIENTO-STUFFED, sliced	2-1/2 cups
MILK	2-1/2 cups
WORCESTERSHIRE SAUCE	3 tablespoons
LIQUID HOT PEPPER SEASONING	1/8 teaspoon

Procedure

Combine all ingredients. Heat just below boiling, stirring constantly.

MUSHROOM HERB SAUCE

Yield: 28 2-ounce portions

Ingredients

CREAM OF MUSHROOM SOUP, CONDENSED	1 50-ounce can
MILK	1-1/4 cups
THYME, POWDERED	1/4 teaspoon

Procedure

Pour soup into saucepan; stir until smooth. Blend in milk and thyme; heat slowly to develop flavors. Serve over open-faced sliced beef sandwiches on toasted buns.

PIMIENTO SAUCE

Yield: 28 2-ounce portions

Ingredients

CREAM OF CHICKEN SOUP, CONDENSED	1 50-ounce can
MILK	1-1/4 cups
PIMIENTO, diced	1-1/4 cups

Procedure

Pour soup into saucepan; stir until smooth. Blend in milk and pimiento; heat. Serve over open-faced chicken or turkey sandwiches on toast. Garnish with toasted almonds, if desired.

PARSLEY SAUCE

Yield: 32 2-ounce portions

Ingredients

CREAM OF CELERY SOUP, CONDENSED	1 50-ounce can
MILK	2 cups
PARSLEY, minced	1/4 cup

Procedure

Pour soup into saucepan; stir until smooth. Blend in milk and parsley; heat. Serve with croquettes or salmon loaf or over open-faced ham-on-dark rye sandwiches.

VARIED CHEESE SAUCE

Yield: 2 quarts

Ingredients

CREAM OF CELERY SOUP, CONDENSED	1 50-ounce can
MILK	1-1/4 cups
CHEESE, CHEDDAR, shredded	12 ounces

Procedure

1. Stir soup until smooth; gradually blend in milk. Heat.
2. Add cheese, stirring constantly until cheese is melted. *Do not boil.*

Note

Vary by adding 2 tablespoons prepared mustard, 1/3 cup chopped pimiento-stuffed olives or 1 cup diced tomatoes.

Bacon Sandwich with Cheese Sauce and Pickles

National Sandwich Idea Contest

Meat Sauces

Glazed Ham with Orange and Cherry Garnish

National Cherry Growers and Industries Foundation

WINE SAUCE FOR HAM

Yield: approximately 1 quart

Ingredients

CURRANT JELLY	1 cup
BEEF STOCK or CONSOMME	1 quart
FLOUR	2 tablespoons
WATER	1/2 cup
SHERRY	2 to 4 tablespoons

Procedure

1. Add the jelly to the stock or consomme; bring to a boil.
2. Blend flour and water; add to boiling liquid. Cook, stirring, until thickened and clear.
3. Add sherry to taste.

SHERRY CHERRY SAUCE FOR HAM

Yield: 1-1/2 quarts; 24 portions

Ingredients

CORNSTARCH	1/3 cup
DRY MUSTARD	1 tablespoon
SALT	2 teaspoons
HAM DRIPPINGS	1/4 cup
WATER	3 cups
SUGAR	3/4 cup
HONEY, STRAINED	1/4 cup
MARASCHINO CHERRIES, sliced	2 cups (14 ounces)
VINEGAR	3 tablespoons
SHERRY	1 cup

Procedure

1. Combine cornstarch, mustard, salt, and ham drippings thoroughly. Add water, sugar, and honey. Bring to a boil; cook, stirring constantly, until mixture is clear and slightly thickened.

2. Add cherries, vinegar, and sherry; blend well. Reheat to boiling point. Serve hot with ham.

RAISIN SAUCE FOR HAM

Yield: 24 2-ounce portions

Ingredients

RAISINS, LIGHT or DARK	2 cups
CORNSTARCH	3 tablespoons
DRY MUSTARD	1 tablespoon
SALT	2 teaspoons
HAM DRIPPINGS	1/4 cup
WATER	1 quart
SUGAR, BROWN, firmly packed	1 cup
VINEGAR	2 tablespoons
LEMON JUICE	3 tablespoons

Procedure

1. Rinse raisins; drain.

2. Blend cornstarch, mustard, and salt into ham drippings. Add water, brown sugar, and raisins. Cook, stirring, until clear and slightly thickened.

3. Blend in vinegar and lemon juice. Serve hot.

APPLE-RAISIN SAUCE

Yield: 24 1/4-cup portions

Ingredients

CORNSTARCH	1/4 cup
SUGAR, BROWN	1/2 cup (3 ounces)
SALT	1/2 teaspoon
ALLSPICE	1/2 teaspoon
APPLE JUICE	1 quart
RAISINS, SEEDLESS	1 cup
APPLES, CANNED, DICED	2 cups

Procedure

1. In saucepan, mix cornstarch, brown sugar, salt, and allspice. Blend in apple juice.

2. Heat, stirring, until mixture comes to a boil. Add raisins. Continue to cook until sauce is clear.

3. Add apples; heat through. Serve over turkey, ham, or smoked tongue.

RED CHERRY SAUCE

Yield: approximately 6 quarts

Ingredients

CHERRIES, RED, SOUR, PITTED	2 No. 10 cans
SUGAR	6 pounds
ALLSPICE	3/4 teaspoon
CORNSTARCH	1-1/2 cups
RED TABLE WINE	3 cups

Procedure

1. Combine cherries and sugar. Heat and stir until sugar is dissolved. Bring to a gentle boil.

2. Blend allspice, cornstarch, and red wine. Add to cherries. Cook, stirring constantly, until sauce thickens and boils.

3. Serve hot over roast or broiled duckling.

MINTED APPLESAUCE

Yield: 3 quarts

Ingredients

APPLESAUCE	1 No. 10 can
LEMON JUICE, fresh	1/4 cup
MINT LEAVES, FRESH, chopped	1-1/4 cups
	(2-1/2 ounces)

Procedure

Combine applesauce, lemon juice, and chopped mint; chill.

ORANGE SAUCE FOR DUCKLING A L'ORANGE

Yield: 2 cups sauce

Ingredients

CHICKEN STOCK	1 cup
ARROWROOT or CORNSTARCH	1 teaspoon
SUGAR	3 tablespoons
WATER	3 tablespoons
ORANGE PEEL, cut julienne, blanched	1 tablespoon
ORANGE JUICE	1/2 cup
LEMON JUICE	1 tablespoon
CURACAO	2 tablespoons

Procedure

1. Skim fat from pan juices from roasting duck. Add 3/4 cup of the chicken stock, scraping all the crusty bits and stirring to dissolve.

2. Mix starch with remainder of stock. Add to hot liquid; cook and stir until clear.

3. In another pan, blend sugar and water; cook until caramelized to a light brown.

4. Combine with the thickened sauce. Add orange peel, orange and lemon juices, and Curacao. Correct seasoning.

SWEET-SOUR SAUCE

Yield: 48 portions

Ingredients

SUGAR, BROWN, firmly packed	1-1/4 cups
CORNSTARCH	3/4 cup
SALT	2 teaspoons
BUTTER or MARGARINE, melted	3/4 cup
PINEAPPLE CHUNKS	1 No. 10 can
PINEAPPLE SYRUP and WATER to equal	1-1/4 quarts
VINEGAR	1-1/3 cups
SOY SAUCE	1/3 cup
PIMIENTO, cut in strips	2-1/2 cups
GREEN PEPPER, cut in 1/4-inch strips	1-1/2 quarts

Procedure

1. Blend brown sugar, cornstarch, and salt into melted butter.
2. Drain pineapple chunks, reserving syrup. Add pineapple syrup and water to brown sugar mixture. Cook, stirring, until thickened and clear.
3. Add pineapple chunks, vinegar, soy sauce, and pimiento. Heat.
4. Add green pepper; heat briefly (green pepper should remain crisp).

LEMON-HONEY SAUCE FOR VEAL CUTLETS OR CHOPS

Yield: 1-3/4 quarts

Ingredients

ORANGE PEEL, freshly grated	1/2 cup
ORANGE JUICE, freshly squeezed	3 cups
LEMON PEEL, freshly grated	3 tablespoons
LEMON JUICE, freshly squeezed	2 cups
HONEY	1 cup
PARSLEY, FRESH, chopped	1 cup
OLIVE OIL	1/2 cup
GARLIC, crushed	4 cloves
CORIANDER, GROUND	1 tablespoon
SALT	1 teaspoon

Procedure

1. Combine all ingredients in a saucepan.
2. Bring to a boil. Reduce heat; simmer 10 minutes.

ROYAL PLUM-RAISIN SAUCE

Yield: 1 quart; 16 2-ounce portions

Ingredients

PURPLE PLUMS	32 (2 No. 2-1/2 cans)
PURPLE PLUM SYRUP	2-1/2 cups
SUGAR	3/4 cup
RAISINS	1-1/2 cups
VINEGAR	1/3 cup
CLOVES, GROUND	1/2 teaspoon
NUTMEG	1/4 teaspoon
MUSTARD	1 tablespoon
LEMON JUICE	1/4 cup

Procedure

1. Drain plums, reserving syrup. Combine syrup, sugar, raisins, vinegar, cloves, nutmeg, mustard, and lemon juice. Bring to a boil; simmer 5 minutes.

2. Serve over cooked ham or Canadian bacon. Garnish each portion with 2 purple plums.

MUSTARD HAM SAUCE

Yield: 2 quarts

Ingredients

PREPARED MUSTARD	1 quart
BUTTER or MARGARINE	1/2 pound
WHITE VINEGAR	1/4 cup
SUGAR, BROWN	1/4 cup
CLOVES, GROUND	1 teaspoon

Procedure

1. Mix all ingredients and simmer for 5 minutes.

2. Serve at room temperature.

Variations

1. Use 1 teaspoon cinnamon in place of ground cloves.

2. Omit cloves. Add a dash of cayenne pepper.

SWEET AND TANGY MUSTARD SAUCE

Yield: 1 gallon

Ingredients

SUGAR	1-1/4 pounds
EGGS, slightly beaten	24 (1-1/4 quarts)
SALT	2 tablespoons
PREPARED MUSTARD	1-1/2 cups
WORCESTERSHIRE SAUCE	1/4 cup
MILK	1-1/2 quarts
LEMON JUICE	2-1/2 cups
LEMON PEEL, grated	1 tablespoon

Procedure

1. Combine sugar, eggs, salt, prepared mustard, Worcestershire sauce, and milk in top of double boiler.

2. Gradually add lemon juice and peel. Cook, stirring, over hot water until sauce thickens.

3. Remove from heat. Cool.

4. Serve with cold sliced ham or pork, hot baked ham, ham loaf, etc.

HONEY-MUSTARD GLAZE FOR LAMB

Yield: 2 cups

Ingredients

PREPARED MUSTARD	1 cup
HONEY	1 cup
SALT	1 teaspoon
BLACK PEPPER	1/2 teaspoon

Procedure

1. Combine all ingredients; blend. Heat over low heat until mixture thickens slightly.

2. Use to baste lamb roasts while cooking or serve as a sauce with lamb.

LEMON-HORSERADISH SAUCE
(for roast beef, veal, or pork)

Yield: 1 quart

Ingredients

LEMON PEEL, grated	1 teaspoon
LEMON JUICE	1/3 cup
PREPARED HORSERADISH	4 ounces
SALT	1/2 teaspoon
CORN SYRUP, LIGHT	1-1/2 tablespoons
CREAM, WHIPPING	2 cups

Procedure

1. Mix lemon peel, lemon juice, horseradish, salt, and corn syrup.
2. Whip cream.
3. Carefully fold horseradish mixture into cream. Chill until ready to serve.

CATSUP AND HORSERADISH SAUCE

Yield: approximately 2-1/4 quarts

Ingredients

BUTTER or MARGARINE	1/2 pound
FLOUR	1/2 cup
CATSUP	2-1/2 cups
WATER	5-1/2 cups
HORSERADISH	1 cup

Procedure

Melt butter in saucepan. Add flour; stir until blended. Add catsup and water gradually. Cook, stirring, until mixture is thickened. Add horseradish.

GOURMET BASTING SAUCE
(for steaks and chops)

Yield: 1 quart

Ingredients

LEMON JUICE	1-1/2 cups
OLIVE OIL or other SALAD OIL	1-1/2 cups
MARJORAM, GROUND	2 tablespoons
BLACK PEPPER, freshly ground	1/2 teaspoon
SALT	2 tablespoons
WORCESTERSHIRE SAUCE	1 cup
GARLIC, pureed	2 cloves

Procedure

1. Blend together all ingredients. Let stand, covered, in refrigerator several hours or overnight.

2. Use to brush steaks or chops while broiling.

ONION RELISH SAUCE

Yield: 2-1/4 quarts

Ingredients

ONION, WHITE, minced	2 pounds
COOKING OIL	1 cup
CATSUP	1 quart
SWEET PICKLE RELISH	1 cup
LEMON JUICE	4 tablespoons
SUGAR	2 tablespoons

Procedure

1. Saute minced onion in oil.

2. Add remaining ingredients; simmer for 15 minutes. Serve the sauce at room temperature.

Dessert Sauces

THE FLOURISH of a well-chosen sauce makes a good dessert a better one.

Suiting a sauce to a dessert involves both character and flavor. In general, a simple sauce is appropriate for a rich dessert, and a rich sauce balances the score for a plainer one. Pleasing contrasts of color are another consideration. A pale, creamy sauce will set off a dessert of a dark brown hue. By the same token, a bright red sauce will enliven a dessert that has very little color of its own.

Dessert sauces are expected to be sweet. But other than that, the characteristics of dessert sauces are quite dissimilar. Some are cooked, others uncooked; some are served hot, others chilled. Some sauces are creamy, some fluffy, others sparkling and clear. Despite the endless variations, most dessert sauces stem from a few basic sauces including custard (or vanilla) sauce, sabayon sauce, fruit sauce, and the syrup type. (We have chosen to classify sabayon sauce with others labeled "spirited.")

Vanilla or custard sauce is the foundation for any number of sweet sauces. It responds to enrichment with cream or additional egg yolk. It also takes to additions, such as fruit, toasted almonds, and whipped cream (which is folded in). Flavorings in harmony with custard sauce include almond, lemon, sherry, brandy, and bourbon, in addition to vanilla, the classic one. Custard sauce and its variations team well with dessert souffles, gelatin desserts, cobblers, and fruit.

Sabayon sauce and other similar sauces consist of egg yolks beaten light with sugar. A typical sabayon sauce includes a wine such as sherry or Marsala and perhaps a soupcon of rum or kirsch. It demands careful cooking over hot water and is served warm over souffles, warm baked apples, steamed puddings, and other hot desserts.

Fruit sauces take many forms and go with all manner of desserts. Some are merely crushed, sweetened berries. Others are slightly thickened, cooked mixtures that may be glistening and clear or they may support pieces of one or more kinds of fruit. Related to the fruit sauces are the melted jellies and other simple sauces of preserves.

Hard sauces are made with butter, confectioners' sugar, and flavoring. They also can accept an addition of fruit. Hard sauce goes well with steamed puddings and hot mincemeat or apple pie. Its use can be extended as well to include fruit crisps, hot baked peach halves, warm spiced applesauce, and such.

Chocolate and butterscotch sauces are familiar examples of the syrup type. These sauces usually take kindly to additions of nuts and are well known for complementing ice cream and a wide variety of other desserts.

Rice Pudding with Dessert Sauce

Rice Council

Fruit Sauces

FRESH BLUEBERRY SAUCE

Yield: 1-1/4 quarts

Ingredients

BLUEBERRIES, FRESH	2 quarts
SUGAR	2 cups
LEMON JUICE	3 tablespoons
SALT	1/4 teaspoon
VANILLA EXTRACT	3/4 teaspoon
LEMON PEEL, grated	1/4 teaspoon

Procedure

1. Wash berries; drain. Crush slightly to start the flow of juice.
2. Add sugar, lemon juice, and salt. Bring to a boil; cook 2 to 3 minutes.
3. Remove from heat. Add vanilla extract and lemon peel. Chill.

Note

If blueberries are very juicy, blend 1 tablespoon cornstarch with the sugar before adding to berries.

SPICED BLUEBERRY SAUCE

Yield: 1 quart

Ingredients

BLUEBERRIES, FRESH or FROZEN	1 quart
JUICE from CANNED PEACHES	3 cups
CORNSTARCH	1-1/2 tablespoons
SUGAR	1 cup
CLOVES, GROUND	1/8 teaspoon
SALT	1/4 teaspoon
LEMON JUICE	1 tablespoon

Procedure

1. Add blueberries to peach juice; bring to a boil.
2. Combine cornstarch, sugar, cloves, and salt, mixing well. Add to hot blueberries, stirring constantly until mixture is thickened and clear.
3. Remove from heat. Add lemon juice. Chill.

LEMON MEDLEY SAUCE

Yield: 2 quarts

Ingredients

LEMON PEEL, grated	3 tablespoons
LEMON JUICE, fresh	1-1/2 cups
SUGAR	1-1/2 quarts
BUTTER	1 pound, 2 ounces
EGGS, slightly beaten	1-1/2 cups

Procedure

1. Combine lemon peel, lemon juice, sugar, and butter. Cook, stirring, over low heat until butter is melted and sugar dissolved.

2. Remove from heat; stir vigorously. Blend 2 cups of mixture into eggs; return all to saucepan. Cook over low heat, stirring constantly, until mixture is thick. Do not boil.

3. Serve over prune whip, baked apples, pears, ice cream, puddings, etc.

LEMON DESSERT SAUCE

Yield: approximately 1 gallon

Ingredients

SUGAR	3 pounds
CORNSTARCH	3/4 cup
LEMON PEEL, grated	2 tablespoons
WATER, cold	2 cups
WATER, boiling	2-1/2 quarts
LEMON JUICE, fresh	1-1/2 cups
BUTTER or MARGARINE	6 ounces
SALT	1 teaspoon
NUTMEG (optional)	1 teaspoon

Procedure

1. Combine sugar, cornstarch, and grated lemon peel. Add cold water; stir until smooth.

2. Add about 1 cup of boiling water to the cornstarch mixture, mixing well. Stirring constantly, pour sauce into remaining boiling water.

3. Boil until thickened, stirring constantly. Remove from heat. Add lemon juice, butter, salt, and nutmeg. Stir until butter melts. Serve over gingerbread, cobblers, Dutch apple pie, puddings, etc.

RICH ORANGE SAUCE

Yield: approximately 1-1/2 quarts

Ingredients

SUGAR	2 cups
CORNSTARCH	6 tablespoons
SALT	1 teaspoon
MACE, GROUND	2 teaspoons
WATER, hot	2 cups
ORANGE JUICE	2 cups
LEMON JUICE	1/2 cup
EGG YOLKS, LARGE, beaten	4
ORANGE PEEL, grated	2 teaspoons
LEMON PEEL, grated	2 teaspoons
BUTTER or MARGARINE	3/4 cup (6 ounces)

Procedure

1. Combine sugar, cornstarch, salt, and mace. Add hot water. Cook, stirring, over moderate heat until thickened.

2. Mix fruit juices with egg yolks. Add a small amount of hot mixture; blend. Stirring constantly, gradually add the egg mixture to the hot cornstarch mixture. Cook and stir until slightly thickened.

3. Blend in grated peels and butter.

SPARKLING CRANBERRY SAUCE

Yield: 6-1/2 cups

Ingredients

CRANBERRY JUICE	1 quart
CORN SYRUP, LIGHT	1-1/2 cups
LEMON JUICE	1/2 cup
FLOUR	3/4 cup
SUGAR	2-1/2 cups

Procedure

1. Combine cranberry juice, corn syrup, and lemon juice; heat.

2. Combine flour and sugar; add to hot liquid; boil about 5 minutes.

3. Serve hot over berry, cherry, or apple pie.

ORANGE FOAMY SAUCE

Yield: 1 quart

Ingredients

ORANGE JUICE, fresh	1 cup
LEMON JUICE, fresh	2 teaspoons
ORANGE PEEL, grated	2 tablespoons
SUGAR, GRANULATED	1/4 cup
CORNSTARCH	2 teaspoons
WATER, cold	2 tablespoons
EGG WHITES	6 (3/4 cup)
SALT	1/8 teaspoon
SUGAR, CONFECTIONERS'	1 cup

Procedure

1. Combine orange and lemon juices, orange peel, and granulated sugar in a saucepan. Bring to a boil.

2. Blend cornstarch with cold water; beat into hot mixture. Cook slowly, stirring, until the sauce clears, 2 to 3 minutes. Cool.

3. Beat egg whites with salt until they form soft peaks. Gradually add confectioners' sugar, beating until thick.

4. Add orange juice mixture slowly, beating until thoroughly blended.

STRAWBERRY SAUCE

Yield: 1-1/4 gallons

Ingredients

GELATIN, STRAWBERRY FLAVOR	1-3/4 cups (12 ounces)
WATER, hot	2 quarts
STRAWBERRIES, FROZEN, SLICED, undrained	6-1/2 pounds

Procedure

Dissolve gelatin in hot water. Add berries. Chill until ready to serve.

Note

If sauce becomes too thick, let stand at room temperature a few minutes before serving.

STRAWBERRY SAUCE SUPREME

Yield: approximately 2-1/4 quarts

Ingredients

STRAWBERRIES, FROZEN, SLICED	4 pounds
ORANGE PEEL, grated	1 tablespoon
ORANGE JUICE	1-1/2 cups
CORNSTARCH	3 tablespoons
SALT	dash
CINNAMON STICKS, 1-1/2-inch	3
MAPLE EXTRACT	1 teaspoon

Procedure

1. Drain strawberries, reserving syrup.
2. Combine syrup, orange peel, orange juice, cornstarch, salt, and cinnamon sticks. Cook and stir over low heat until thickened and clear. Remove cinnamon sticks.
3. Cool slightly; add maple extract and berries.

Note

Suggested as sauce for white cake layers which have been topped with strawberry ice cream.

CHERRY-PINEAPPLE SAUCE

Yield: 1 gallon

Ingredients

CHERRIES, FROZEN, RED, SOUR, PITTED	
(packed 5 parts cherries to 1 part sugar)	5 pounds
PINEAPPLE TIDBITS, undrained	1 quart
	(2-1/4 pounds)
CHERRY and PINEAPPLE JUICE	1 quart
GELATIN, ORANGE FLAVOR	1-1/2 pounds
SALT	1-1/2 teaspoons
CORN SYRUP, LIGHT	1 quart

Procedure

1. Thaw cherries. Drain cherries and pineapple, reserving juices.
2. Measure 1 quart of the combined juices; bring to a boil; pour over gelatin and salt. Stir until dissolved. Add corn syrup and drained fruits. Chill until ready to serve.

Eye-catching Ice Cream Desserts with Wafer Garnish

California Apricot Advisory Board; National Cherry Growers & Industries Foundation; Sunkist Growers, Inc.

FOAMY STRAWBERRY SAUCE

Yield: approximately 2-1/2 quarts

Ingredients

BUTTER or MARGARINE	6 ounces
FLOUR	3 tablespoons
SUGAR	1-1/2 cups
STRAWBERRIES, FROZEN, SLICED, thawed	2 pounds
LEMON JUICE	3 tablespoons
KIRSCH or COINTREAU	1/3 cup
EGG WHITES	3
CREAM, HEAVY	1-1/2 cups

Procedure

1. Melt butter; add flour and sugar. Cook, stirring, over hot water or very low heat until smooth and thickened, 5 to 10 minutes.

2. Puree berries. Add to butter mixture. Add lemon juice. Continue to cook, stirring, until thickened. Remove from heat. Cool. Add the liqueur.

3. Beat egg whites until stiff and shiny.

4. Whip cream.

5. Fold egg whites into berry mixture; fold in cream.

Note

Suggested to serve over strawberry snowballs (balls of strawberry ice cream rolled in flaked coconut).

HONEY-LIME-GINGER SAUCE

Yield: approximately 1-1/2 quarts

Ingredients

SYRUP from CANNED PEARS	2 cups
HONEY	2 cups
LIME JUICE	1 cup
CRYSTALLIZED GINGER, slivered	1/2 cup
LIMES, thinly sliced, cut into segments	2

Procedure

1. Combine pear syrup, honey, and lime juice.

2. Add ginger and lime segments; mix well.

3. Serve over drained, chilled pear halves.

RUM-SHERRY-PRUNE SAUCE

Yield: 2 quarts

Ingredients

PRUNES, WHOLE, DRIED	2 pounds
WATER	2 quarts
PRUNE LIQUID	2 cups
SUGAR	1 cup
CINNAMON, GROUND	1 teaspoon
SHERRY, SWEET	1 cup
RUM, LIGHT or DARK, as preferred	1/4 cup
ALMONDS, SLIVERED	1 cup

Procedure

1. Cover prunes with cold water; soak in refrigerator overnight. Drain, reserving 2 cups liquid.

2. Pit prunes; cut fruit into quarters.

3. Combine prune liquid, sugar, and cinnamon. Bring to a boil; simmer at least 5 minutes.

4. Remove from heat. Add prunes, sherry, rum, and almonds. Chill.

5. Use as a sauce for ice cream.

RED CHERRY SAUCE

Yield: 1-1/4 quarts

Ingredients

CHERRIES, FROZEN, TART, thawed	1 quart
WATER	1 cup
SUGAR	1/2 cup
CORNSTARCH	2 tablespoons
LEMON JUICE	2 teaspoons
RED FOOD COLORING (optional)	few drops

Procedure

1. Drain cherries, reserving juice; add water to juice.

2. Combine sugar and cornstarch; stir into liquid mixture. Heat, stirring, until thickened and clear.

3. Add cherries, lemon juice, and, if desired, red food coloring.

SAUCE TAHITI

Yield: 2 quarts

Ingredients

BANANAS, RIPE, mashed	1-1/2 cups
LEMON JUICE	3 tablespoons
ORANGE MARMALADE	1-1/2 pounds
PINEAPPLE PRESERVES	1-1/2 pounds
MARASCHINO CHERRIES, drained, chopped	1-1/2 pounds
COCONUT, toasted	as needed

Procedure

1. Combine bananas and lemon juice.
2. Add marmalade and preserves. Cook slowly, stirring constantly, for 5 minutes.
3. Add maraschino cherries.
4. Serve warm over vanilla or cherry vanilla ice cream, pineapple, or orange sherbet. Sprinkle sundaes with toasted coconut.

MELBA SAUCE

Yield: approximately 1 quart

Ingredients

CORNSTARCH	1/4 cup
SALT	1/4 teaspoon
WATER	1/4 cup
RASPBERRIES, FROZEN	2-1/2 pounds
RED CURRANT JELLY	2 cups

Procedure

1. Blend cornstarch, salt, and water. Add raspberries and jelly.
2. Bring to a boil, stirring constantly. Reduce heat; simmer about 5 minutes, stirring as needed.
3. Sieve or strain mixture; chill.

NUTMEG PINEAPPLE SAUCE

Yield: approximately 1 quart

Ingredients

SUGAR	1 cup
CORNSTARCH	1/4 cup
SALT	1/2 teaspoon
NUTMEG, GROUND	1 teaspoon
PINEAPPLE, CRUSHED, undrained	1 quart
LEMON JUICE	1/4 cup
VANILLA	1 tablespoon

Procedure

1. Combine sugar, cornstarch, salt, and nutmeg. Add pineapple and lemon juice; mix well.
2. Cook over moderate heat, stirring constantly, until sauce clears and thickens, about 3 minutes.
3. Remove from heat; add vanilla. Cool.

PEACH MELBA SAUCE

Yield: approximately 1-1/2 quarts

Ingredients

KIRSCHWASSER or COINTREAU	6 tablespoons
PEACHES, CANNED, SLICED, drained	2 cups
RASPBERRIES or BOYSENBERRIES, CANNED, drained	1 cup
VANILLA ICE CREAM	1 quart

Procedure

1. Pour liqueur over peaches and berries; chill.
2. Soften ice cream; stir until whipped cream consistency. Quickly fold in the fruits.
3. Serve immediately over fruits, angel food or plain cake, or ice cream.

GINGERED PEACH SAUCE

Yield: 2 quarts

Ingredients

WATER	1 cup
SUGAR, BROWN, firmly packed	1 cup
SALT	1/8 teaspoon
CORNSTARCH	2 tablespoons
WATER	1/2 cup
PEACHES, CANNED, SOLID PACK, SLICED, UNSWEETENED	6-1/4 cups
CANDIED GINGER, slivered	2 tablespoons

Procedure

1. Combine first amount of water with brown sugar and salt in the top of a 3-quart double boiler.

2. Blend cornstarch with second amount of water; add to sugar mixture.

3. Bring to a boil over direct heat, stirring constantly until thickened. Set over hot water.

4. Add peaches and ginger; heat for 10 minutes.

5. Serve hot or cold over angel food or pound cake a la mode.

TROPICAL FRUIT SAUCE

Yield: approximately 2 quarts

Ingredients

PINEAPPLE TIDBITS	1-3/4 quarts
SUGAR, BROWN, firmly packed	1 cup
LEMON JUICE	2 tablespoons
BANANAS, diced	2 cups
NUTS, coarsely chopped	1 cup
RUM, DARK	1 to 1-1/4 cups

Procedure

1. Drain pineapple, reserving syrup. Combine syrup, brown sugar, and lemon juice. Boil until reduced to half its original volume. Remove from heat.

2. Add pineapple, bananas, nuts, and rum. Chill.

3. Serve over coffee, vanilla, or strawberry ice cream or on custards, plain puddings, or whipped cream-topped slices of angel food cake.

CHINESE CITRUS SAUCE

Yield: 3-1/2 quarts

Ingredients

ORANGE SECTIONS, FRESH, diced	2 cups
GRAPEFRUIT SECTIONS, FRESH, diced	2 cups
PINEAPPLE, FRESH, diced	2 cups
WATER	1-1/2 quarts
ORANGE JUICE	1 quart
LEMON JUICE	1 cup
SUGAR	3 cups
SALT	1/2 teaspoon
ARROWROOT or CORNSTARCH	3/4 cup
WATER	3/4 cup

Procedure

1. Prepare fruit; set aside.

2. Combine first amount of water, orange juice, lemon juice, sugar, and salt. Bring to a boil; simmer 3 to 5 minutes.

3. Blend starch with second amount of water to make a smooth paste. Add to hot liquid; cook, stirring, until thickened and clear.

4. Remove from heat; fold in fruit.

FIVE FRUIT SAUCE

Yield: approximately 2-1/2 quarts

Ingredients

FRUIT COCKTAIL	1 No. 10 can
SUGAR	2 cups
ORANGE PEEL, DRIED	1/2 cup
LEMON JUICE	1 teaspoon
TRIPLE SEC or CURACAO	1 cup

Procedure

1. Drain fruit cocktail, reserving syrup. Combine syrup, sugar, orange peel, and lemon juice. Boil until reduced to half its original volume.

2. Add fruit and Triple Sec; heat.

3. Serve hot over rolled dessert pancakes or on puddings or ice cream.

Note

If desired, warm additional Triple Sec; set aflame; pour over the dessert pancakes.

VINEYARD MINCEMEAT SAUCE ⟶

Yield: 1 quart

Ingredients

CORNSTARCH	2 tablespoons
SUGAR, BROWN, firmly packed	1/2 cup
SALT	dash
MUSCATEL, ANGELICA, or other DESSERT WINE	1 cup
WATER	1 cup
MINCEMEAT, PREPARED	2 cups
BUTTER or MARGARINE	2 tablespoons
LEMON JUICE	2 tablespoons
LEMON PEEL, grated	2 teaspoons

JEWELLED DESSERT SAUCE

Yield: 5 quarts

Ingredients

FRUIT COCKTAIL	1 No. 10 can
CRANBERRY JUICE COCKTAIL	2 quarts
CORNSTARCH	1 cup (5 ounces)
SALT	1 teaspoon
VANILLA	2 teaspoons
RED FOOD COLORING (optional)	as needed

Procedure

1. Drain fruit cocktail, reserving syrup. Pour syrup into a large saucepan.

2. Mix a little cranberry juice cocktail with cornstarch. Add to saucepan; add remaining cranberry juice cocktail. Cook and stir until thickened.

3. Remove from heat; add fruit cocktail, salt, and vanilla. If desired, tint with red food coloring to produce a slightly deeper shade. Chill.

4. Use as sauce for white cake layers which have been topped with vanilla ice cream and sprinkled with coconut. Or, use on balls of ice cream rolled in coconut or on scoops of vanilla ice cream.

Procedure

1. Mix cornstarch, brown sugar, and salt. Add wine and water gradually, stirring until smooth.

2. Bring to a boil over medium heat, stirring until mixture thickens and becomes clear.

3. Add remaining ingredients. Heat thoroughly.

4. Serve over steamed puddings that require a "fruity" sauce, over squares of warm gingerbread or yellow cake, or over vanilla ice cream.

BRANDIED FRUIT SAUCE

Yield: approximately 1 quart

Ingredients

FRUIT COCKTAIL	3-1/2 cups
CINNAMON STICK, 3-inch	1
SUGAR	1/2 cup
CORNSTARCH	3 tablespoons
SALT	1/4 teaspoon
WATER	1/2 cup
LEMON JUICE	1/4 cup
BRANDY	1/3 cup

Procedure

1. Heat fruit cocktail with cinnamon stick to boiling point in covered saucepan.

2. Combine sugar, cornstarch, salt, and water. Stir into fruit. Cook, stirring gently, until mixture thickens and syrup is clear. Remove from heat. Stir in lemon juice and brandy.

3. Serve hot over steamed puddings, fruitcake, gingerbread, pound cake, or ice cream.

FRUITED HARD SAUCE

Yield: 1 quart

Ingredients

RAISINS, DARK or GOLDEN	1/2 cup
MIXED CANDIED FRUITS AND PEELS, finely cut	1/2 cup
BRANDY	3 tablespoons
BUTTER or MARGARINE	6 ounces
SUGAR, CONFECTIONERS'	1 pound
VANILLA	2 teaspoons
CREAM, LIGHT	1 tablespoon

Procedure

1. Chop raisins coarsely. Combine with candied fruits and brandy.
2. Cream butter until soft. Gradually beat in confectioners' sugar, vanilla, and cream until mixture is soft and fluffy.
3. Add fruit mixture. Cover; refrigerate several hours to mellow.

ROSY APPLE DESSERT SAUCE

Yield: 3-1/4 quarts

Ingredients

APPLE SLICES, drained	1 No. 10 can
RED CINNAMON CANDIES	2-1/2 cups
SUGAR	2-1/2 cups

Procedure

1. Combine all ingredients; bring to a boil.
2. Cover; simmer 15 minutes. Chill.
3. Serve over ice cream, pudding, or custard. Or, layer with ice cream in parfait dishes.

CANNED FRUIT TOPPING

Yield: approximately 50 portions

Ingredients

FRUIT, WATER PACK	1 No. 10 can
FRUIT JUICE	3 cups
CORNSTARCH	1/2 cup
SUGAR	3 cups
SALT	1-1/2 teaspoons
LEMON JUICE	2 tablespoons

Procedure

1. Drain fruit, reserving juice. Heat 2 cups of juice to boiling. Mix one cup of cold juice with cornstarch; add, while stirring, to hot juice. Cook until thickened and clear.

2. Stir sugar, salt, and lemon juice into thickened juice.

3. Add drained fruit, mixing gently. Cool. Use as a fruit topping over sliced cake, puddings, custards, etc.

Blueberry, Raspberry, Boysenberry Topping: If desired, add 1 teaspoon cinnamon with the sugar.

Cherry Topping: Use red, tart, pitted cherries. If desired, add 1 teaspoon red food coloring to thickened juice before adding fruit.

Peach Topping: Use sliced peaches for fruit.

Pineapple Topping: Use crushed pineapple or tidbits for fruit.

Melon Balls with Coconut Garnish

Western Growers Association

Custard Sauces

CUSTARD CREAM SAUCE

Yield: approximately 1 quart

Ingredients

CREAM, LIGHT	2 cups
EGGS	3
SALT	1/8 teaspoon
SUGAR	1/3 cup
PORT	1/2 cup
ALMONDS, BLANCHED, SLIVERED, toasted	1/2 cup
CREAM, WHIPPING	1 cup

Procedure

1. Scald light cream over hot water.

2. Beat eggs lightly with salt and sugar. Stir a small amount of the hot cream into the mixture. Combine with remaining cream; cook, stirring constantly, until mixture thickens and coats spoon.

3. Remove from heat; cool thoroughly.

4. Add port and almonds.

5. Whip cream until barely stiff. Fold into custard mixture just before serving.

6. Serve on baked custards, over fresh or canned fruits, pound cake, or angel food slices.

RICH CUSTARD SAUCE

Yield: 1-1/4 quarts

Ingredients

MILK	1 quart
SUGAR	1/4 cup
EGG YOLKS	10
SUGAR	1/4 cup
SALT	1/4 teaspoon
VANILLA	1 teaspoon
CREAM, LIGHT or HEAVY	1/2 cup

Procedure

1. Scald milk with the first amount of sugar.

2. Beat egg yolks slightly, adding second amount of sugar and the salt.

3. Stirring constantly, slowly add hot milk to egg mixture. Cook in a double boiler or over low heat, stirring constantly, until the mixture coats a spoon.

4. Remove from heat; place pan in a container of cold water.

5. Add vanilla and cream; stir until slightly cooled.

6. Chill. Serve on fresh berries, peaches, orange sections, sliced bananas, plain gelatin, and other desserts.

ALMOND CUSTARD SAUCE

Yield: 5 quarts

Ingredients

SUGAR	14 ounces
CORNSTARCH	2 ounces
SALT	1/2 teaspoon
MILK, cold	2 cups
MILK, hot	3 quarts
EGG YOLKS, beaten	10 (7 ounces)
ALMOND EXTRACT	2 tablespoons

Procedure

1. Mix sugar, cornstarch, and salt. Add cold milk; blend.

2. Add hot milk, stirring constantly. Add beaten egg yolks slowly, stirring constantly. Blend well.

3. Cook over hot water, continuing to stir until custard is slightly thickened and coats a metal spoon. Remove from heat; add almond extract. Cool quickly. Chill.

TOASTED ALMOND SAUCE

Yield: 3 cups; 24 1-ounce portions

Ingredients

WATER	1-1/2 cups
NONFAT DRY MILK	3/4 cup
EGGS, beaten	1/2 cup
SUGAR, GRANULATED	1/4 cup
SALT	dash
ALMONDS, SLIVERED, toasted	1/3 cup
SHERRY	2 tablespoons

Procedure

1. Put water in top of a double boiler. Sieve dry milk over water; beat until evenly dissolved.

2. Heat reconstituted milk over hot water.

3. Combine beaten eggs with sugar and salt.

4. Stir a small amount of hot milk into egg mixture; blend. Gradually stir egg mixture into remaining milk.

5. Stirring constantly, cook slowly over hot water just until mixture thickens.

6. Remove from heat; chill.

7. Add almonds and sherry. Serve over wedge of angel food cake.

COTTAGE CHEESE DESSERT SAUCE

Yield: 1 quart

Ingredients

COTTAGE CHEESE	2 pounds
CREAM, HEAVY	1/4 cup
SUGAR	1/4 cup
VANILLA	2 teaspoons
LEMON PEEL, grated	1 teaspoon

Procedure

1. In a mixer or blender, beat cottage cheese with cream, sugar, vanilla, and lemon peel.

2. Serve over sweetened fresh strawberries, peaches, or blueberries.

Variation

Use brown sugar instead of granulated sugar and substitute 1 teaspoon almond extract for the vanilla. Serve over stewed apricots or sweetened, pitted, fresh dark cherries.

Syrup Type Sauces

BUTTERSCOTCH SAUCE

Yield: approximately 1-3/4 quarts

Ingredients

SUGAR, LIGHT BROWN	1-1/2 pounds
CORN SYRUP, LIGHT	1 cup
BUTTER	1/2 pound
WATER	2 cups
CREAM, LIGHT (18%)	2 cups

Procedure

1. Combine brown sugar, corn syrup, butter, and water. Cook over low heat until syrup reaches a temperature of 232°F.

2. Remove from heat. Blend in cream.

3. Serve warm over vanilla ice cream on slices of angel food cake. Top desserts with a few lightly sauteed whole almonds, if desired.

PRALINE SAUCE

Yield: approximately 3 quarts

Ingredients

BUTTER	1/2 pound
PECANS, BROKEN	1-1/4 pounds
SUGAR, BROWN	1 pound, 6 ounces
CORN SYRUP, LIGHT	1 cup
HALF-AND-HALF or LIGHT CREAM	1 quart
VANILLA	1 tablespoon

Procedure

1. Melt butter; saute pecans until toasted.

2. Add brown sugar and corn syrup; bring to a boil.

3. Gradually blend in half-and-half.

4. Remove from heat. Add vanilla. Serve warm or cold over vanilla or strawberry ice cream.

Note

Sauce may be refrigerated and reheated.

WARM CARAMEL CREAM SAUCE

Yield: 1-1/2 quarts

Ingredients

BUTTER	1/2 pound
SUGAR, LIGHT BROWN	1-1/2 pounds
SOUR CREAM (room temperature)	1 quart
VANILLA	1 tablespoon

Procedure

1. Combine butter and brown sugar in a heavy saucepan. Stirring constantly, cook 2 to 3 minutes or until smooth and syrupy.

2. Remove from heat; cool slightly. Gradually stir in sour cream and vanilla.

3. Serve warm over steamed puddings, fruitcake, apple desserts, gingerbread, or ice cream.

ALMOND TOFFEE SAUCE

Yield: approximately 1 quart

Ingredients

SUGAR, GRANULATED	1 cup
SUGAR, DARK BROWN, firmly packed	1 cup
CREAM, LIGHT	2 cups
BUTTER or MARGARINE	3/4 cup (6 ounces)
SALT	1/2 teaspoon
VANILLA	1 teaspoon
ALMOND EXTRACT	1/4 teaspoon
ALMONDS, SLIVERED, toasted	1 cup

Procedure

1. Combine sugars, cream, butter, and salt.

2. Heat, stirring over medium heat until sugar is dissolved. Bring to a full boil; remove from heat. Cool.

3. Stir in vanilla, almond extract, and almonds.

4. Serve over a compote of canned fruits, such as pears, peaches, pineapple, and apricots.

California Strawberry Advisory Board

Sweetheart Sundaes

Strawberry ice cream in heart-shaped meringue shells topped with marshmallow sauce and garnished with a strawberry.

ICE CREAM SAUCE

Yield: 1-1/4 quarts

Ingredients

EGGS	2
SUGAR, GRANULATED	1/2 cup
SALT	1/4 teaspoon
BUTTER, melted	1/2 cup
VANILLA	2 teaspoons
CREAM, WHIPPING	2 cups

Procedure

1. Beat eggs until thick and light. Beat in sugar and salt.
2. Gradually beat in butter and vanilla.
3. Whip cream until thick and glossy. Fold into egg mixture. Serve on steamed puddings, gingerbread, or warm chocolate cake.

MARSHMALLOW PEPPERMINT SAUCE

Yield: 1 gallon

Ingredients

MARSHMALLOW TOPPING	1 gallon
PEPPERMINT EXTRACT	3 to 4 teaspoons
HALF-AND-HALF or LIGHT CREAM	1 cup
RED FOOD COLORING (optional)	as needed

Procedure

1. Combine marshmallow topping, peppermint extract, and half-and-half; mix well. If desired, add red food coloring to tint a pale pink color. Heat until warm. Do not boil.
2. Serve over vanilla or chocolate ice cream. Top sundae with crushed peppermint candy, if desired.

HOT FUDGE SAUCE

Yield: 2 quarts

Ingredients

CHOCOLATE, UNSWEETENED	1-1/4 pounds
SUGAR	1-1/2 quarts
SALT	1/4 teaspoon
WATER, hot	1 quart

Procedure

1. Melt chocolate in a heavy saucepan *over very low heat.* Add sugar and salt; blend well.

2. Add hot water gradually, stirring constantly until thoroughly blended.

3. Cook, stirring, until sugar is dissolved and mixture comes to a boil. Continue boiling about 15 minutes or until syrup sheets from a spoon like jelly (220°F.).

4. Remove from heat. Keep warm over hot, not boiling, water. Serve warm on ice cream and other desserts.

CHOCOLATE PEANUT BUTTER SAUCE

Yield: 4-1/2 quarts

Ingredients

INSTANT PUDDING, CHOCOLATE	2-1/4 pounds
WATER, cold	2 cups
CORN SYRUP	3 quarts
PEANUT BUTTER, CREAMY	2 cups (1 pound)
MARGARINE, melted	1/2 pound

Procedure

1. Dissolve instant chocolate pudding in water; blend in corn syrup.

2. Slowly blend chocolate mixture into peanut butter. Stir in melted margarine. Serve over ice cream.

Spirited Sauces

ENHANCING THE flavor of a sauce with a wine or brandy is an old, old art. Now, the more adventuresome are rediscovering the culinary talents of cordials, liqueurs, whiskies, and rum. Any one of these spirits can give a marvelous fillip of taste to a sauce which, in turn, can do wonderful things for the dessert it dresses.

When using spirits, be sure that the flavor quality is good. For a liquor of any kind cannot be expected to impart a flavor that is not there. Another important rule: use the light touch; use enough, but only enough, to give the desired result. Too much can ruin the whole effect.

Spirited sauces offer possibilities for dramatic flaming. For a successful flambe, use a brandy, rum, or other liquor with a proof of 50 or more. As the first step, warm the sauce. Then float more of the spirits on top but do not stir in. Or, warm the liquor separately and set it aflame, then pour the blazing liquid into the sauce. Either way, the heat releases the alcohol as vapor, making it easy to ignite.

Cordials and liqueurs, as spirits that are sweet, make ready-to-pour sauces for ice cream, sherbets, custards, and many fruits. There is, for example, a simple elegance to:

Orange sherbet piled in frozen orange shells and sauced with Grand Marnier

Cone-shaped scoops of lemon sherbet topped with Creme de Menthe and garnished with chocolate curls

Ambrosia (made with sliced oranges and moist coconut) marinated with Cointreau or Triple Sec

Raspberry sherbet sauced with Creme de Cassis or Creme de Framboises

Turned-out cups of baked vanilla custard with a sauce of Kahlua and pieces of marrons glace

Butter pecan or burnt almond ice cream splashed with Drambuie

A cluster of small scoops of coffee, chocolate, and vanilla ice cream topped with diced, roasted almonds and Amaretto di Saronno.

Flaming Raisin Sauce

California Raisin Advisory Board

ALMOND RUM SAUCE

Yield: approximately 1 quart

Ingredients

SUGAR, LIGHT BROWN, firmly packed	1-1/2 cups
CORNSTARCH	1/4 cup
SALT	1/4 teaspoon
WATER	1-1/2 cups
ALMONDS, DICED, roasted	3/4 cup
ORANGE PEEL, grated	2 tablespoons
ORANGE JUICE	1 cup
BUTTER or MARGARINE	1/3 cup
RUM	3/4 cup

Procedure

1. Combine sugar, cornstarch, and salt in a heavy saucepan. Blend in water; cook, stirring constantly, until mixture is thickened and clear.

2. Add almonds, orange peel and juice, butter, and rum. Cook until heated through.

3. Serve warm over plum pudding, fruitcake, ice cream, or Baked Alaska.

SABAYON SAUCE

Yield: 2 quarts

Ingredients

EGG YOLKS	16
SUGAR	2 cups
SALT	1/4 teaspoon
LEMON JUICE	1/3 cup
SHERRY	2 cups
BRANDY	1/3 cup
CREAM, WHIPPING	2 cups

Procedure

1. Beat egg yolks until light. Add sugar and salt.

2. Cook in a double boiler, whipping constantly until thick. Gradually add lemon juice, sherry, and brandy; cool.

3. Whip cream; fold into sauce.

4. Serve on fruit cobblers, other fruit desserts, or ice cream.

ZABAGLIONE

Yield: 24 portions

Ingredients

EGG YOLKS	18 (1-1/2 cups)
SUGAR, GRANULATED	4-1/2 cups
LEMON PEEL, grated	3 tablespoons
LEMON JUICE	2/3 cup
SHERRY or MARSALA	3 cups

Procedure

1. Beat egg yolks lightly.

2. Add remaining ingredients; cook over boiling water, beating constantly with wire whip until as thick and fluffy as whipped cream. Remove from heat at once.

3. Serve hot or chilled over sponge cake or fruit.

BOURBON NUTMEG SAUCE

Yield: approximately 1 quart

Ingredients

EGGS	4
SUGAR	1/3 cup
SALT	1/8 teaspoon
MILK	1 quart
BOURBON	1/3 cup
NUTMEG	1/2 teaspoon

Procedure

1. Beat eggs slightly with sugar and salt.

2. Add milk gradually, stirring constantly. Gradually stir in bourbon.

3. Stirring constantly, cook over hot, not boiling, water until mixture coats spoon.

4. Remove from heat; pour into a cool bowl. Add nutmeg. Cover; chill.

5. Serve on warm apple pie, peach cobbler, apple crisp, or baked apples.

BRANDY SAUCE

Yield: 2-1/4 quarts

Ingredients

BUTTER or MARGARINE	1-1/2 cups
SUGAR, CONFECTIONERS'	3 cups
EGG YOLKS	12 (1 cup)
CREAM, HEAVY	1 quart
COGNAC or other BRANDY	6 ounces

Procedure

1. Cream butter with confectioners' sugar.
2. Gradually add and blend in the egg yolks.
3. Combine mixture with cream and cook over hot water, stirring constantly until mixture coats the spoon.
4. Flavor with brandy, increasing amount if desired.

PACIFIC RUM SAUCE

Yield: 3-1/2 quarts

Ingredients

SUGAR	2-1/2 pounds
CORNSTARCH	4 ounces
SALT	1/4 teaspoon
WATER, boiling	2-1/4 quarts
BUTTER or MARGARINE	3 ounces
LEMON PEEL, grated	1/2 ounce
LEMON JUICE	1-1/4 cups
RUM	3 cups

Procedure

1. Combine sugar, cornstarch, and salt; mix thoroughly. Gradually stir into boiling water. Add butter; heat to boiling.
2. Cook 8 to 10 minutes, stirring occasionally. Remove from heat.
3. Add lemon peel and juice and the rum.
4. Serve hot or cold on fruits, puddings, custards, apple cobbler, or other apple desserts.

ROMANOFF SAUCE
(for strawberries or compote of sliced strawberries and canned pineapple)

Yield: 1 quart sauce base

Ingredients

SUGAR	2-1/4 cups
WATER	3 cups
LEMON PEEL, grated	3 tablespoons
LEMON JUICE	1/3 cup
EGG YOLKS	3
SUGAR	3/4 cup
BUTTER or MARGARINE	1/3 cup
RUM, LIGHT	1-1/2 cups
CREAM, WHIPPING	as needed

Procedure

1. Combine first amount of sugar and the water. Cook to a thick syrup (240°F.). Add lemon peel and juice.

2. Beat egg yolks with second amount of sugar. Gradually add to hot syrup. Cook, stirring, over low heat for 5 minutes.

3. Add butter and rum; heat until butter melts. Cool. Cover; chill.

4. Fold rum sauce into whipped cream in proportions to suit taste. (Try 1 cup sauce with 1 cup cream, whipped until stiff.)

RICH SHERRY SAUCE

Yield: 6-1/2 quarts

Ingredients

VANILLA PIE FILLING AND PUDDING MIX	2 cups (14 ounces)
MILK, cold	2 cups
SUGAR	1 cup
MILK, scalded	3-1/2 quarts
SHERRY	1 cup
NUTMEG	1/2 teaspoon
CREAM, WHIPPING	1 quart

Procedure

1. Blend dry pie filling mix with cold milk.

2. Add sugar to scalded milk (heated just below boiling). Stir in pie filling mixture. Stirring constantly, cook over boiling water until mixture thickens, about 3 minutes. Continue cooking 10 minutes longer, stirring frequently.

3. Remove from heat. Chill.

4. Add sherry and nutmeg.

5. Whip cream; fold into sauce.

6. Serve with apple puddings, bread pudding, dessert souffles, or trifles.

CLARET WINE SAUCE

Yield: 3-1/2 quarts

Ingredients

CORNSTARCH	4-1/2 ounces
SUGAR	2-1/4 pounds
SALT	1-1/4 teaspoons
WATER	1-1/4 quarts
CLARET or BURGUNDY	1-1/4 quarts
LEMON JUICE	1-1/2 cups
LEMON PEEL, grated	1/2 ounce
BUTTER or MARGARINE	1/2 pound

Procedure

1. Combine cornstarch, sugar, and salt. Add water and wine gradually, stirring until smooth.

2. Cook over medium heat, stirring until mixture boils. Lower heat; simmer, stirring constantly, for 5 to 8 minutes.

3. Remove from heat. Add lemon juice and peel and the butter; blend.

4. Serve warm or cold on puddings, cakes, pies, fruit compotes, baked apples, and other desserts.

SHERRY SPICE SAUCE

Yield: 25 4-ounce portions

Ingredients

CREAM, LIGHT or HALF-AND-HALF	2-1/2 quarts
CORNSTARCH	3/4 cup
SUGAR	3 cups
CINNAMON	1 teaspoon
NUTMEG	1/2 teaspoon
SALT	1/2 teaspoon
SHERRY	1 cup
LEMON PEEL, grated	1 teaspoon
BUTTER or MARGARINE	4 ounces

Procedure

1. Heat cream.

2. Mix cornstarch, sugar, spices, and salt. Blend in sherry. Add to hot cream; stir well; bring to a boil.

3. Add lemon peel; cook, stirring, for 3 minutes.

4. Remove from heat; blend in butter. Serve warm over apple crisp, apple pie, or apple dumplings.

Dessert Garnishes

Cling Peach Advisory Board

National Cherry Growers & Industries Foundation

INDEX